The

OMEGA-3
Advantage

The OMEGA-3 Advantage

Groundbreaking New Guidelines for Preventing or Lowering Your Risk of Heart Disease, High Blood Pressure, Migraines, Asthma, Cancer, and Arthritis with the Powerful Benefits of Fish Oils

Kristine Napier, M.P.H., R.D., L.D.
with Fiona Hinton, M.N.D., S.R.D.

Produced by The Philip Lief Group, Inc.

BARNES &NOBLE BOOKS
NEW YORK

2004 Barnes & Noble Books

ISBN 0-7607-4248-0

Design: Paul Kezmarsky

Printed and bound in The United States of America

04 05 06 07 08 M 9 8 7 6   5 4 3 2 1

Contents

Introduction: Omega-3s for Healthy Hearts . . . and Much, Much More!!. ix

One More Reason to Eat More Omega-3s . . .
But Do I Have to Eat Fish?
This Book Will Help You to Understand:
Omega-3s to My Rescue—in Six Life-Saving Ways
Fish Fats Swim to My Rescue

Chapter 1: The Omega-3 Story: What Are Omega-3s? How Did We Discover Their Health Benefits? 1

It All Began with a Tall Fish Tale
Just What Are Omega-3 Fats?
Two Essential Fats: Omega-3s and Omega-6s
How Much Omega-3 Does My Body Need?

Chapter 2: The Power of Omega-3 in Heart Disease. 15

Diet and Heart Disease—a Primer
How Omega-3s Protect Your Heart
How Much Omega-3 Do We Need?
Omega-3s: Heart-Healthy for You and Me

Chapter 3: Omega-3s and the Prevention of Other Conditions Affecting the Body and Mind. 31

Omega-3s at the Beginning of Life
Omega-3s and the Power to Calm Inflammation
Omega-3s: Their Role in Mood and Mental Function
Omega-3s: Other Health Benefits
But Wait . . . There'll Be More

Chapter 4: Omega-3 Sources: Thoughts on Supplements and Food Charts 51

The Skinny on Supplements
Safety Issues and Other Concerns
What Information Will I Find in These Charts?

Chapter 5: Reeling in the Basics: Buying, Storing, and Cooking Fish 75

Mercury in Fish: Putting it into Perspective
Getting the Most Omega-3s . . . from the Best Fish
From the Store to Your Dinner Plate: the Facts on Fish
Enjoying More Fish—for Your Heart and Your Tastebuds

Chapter 6: About Non-Fish Sources of Omega-3s 89

Flaxseed
Walnuts . . . Especially English Ones!
Choosing the Best Oil . . . When You Need One
How to Buy, Store, and Cook Arugula, Other Greens, Broccoli,
and Other Vegetables
Help with Buying, Cooking, and Storing Legumes
How to Buy, Store, and Cook Soy Foods
Omega-3 Fats—So Much More than Fish

Chapter 7: A Perspective on Omega-3s—the Whole Picture of a Healthy Lifestyle 105

A Healthy Diet for a Healthy Life
Special Tips for Heart Disease
Special Tips for High Blood Pressure
Special Tips for Type 2 Diabetes
Special Tips for Reducing Cancer Risk
Putting it all Together

Chapter 8: Putting Omega-3s into Practice and onto Your Plate: Mealplans and Recipes 121

Using Our Mealplans and Recipes
Fish Menus
Non-Fish Menus
Recipes

Index **205**

Introduction:

Omega-3s for Healthy Hearts ... and Much, Much More!!

The Eskimos of Greenland eat fish to their hearts' content. Indeed, say experts, generous fish consumption is responsible for their exceedingly low rate of artery-choking heart disease, and maybe even for their decreased chances of suffering adult-onset diabetes. Research from around the world is incredibly consistent in uncovering the same association: death from heart disease is more unusual among people who eat at least some fish than among those who do not. This tells us that, although the Eskimos eat remarkably large amounts of fish, we can all reap the heart health benefits, even with much more moderate amounts of fish.

Advances in nutrition and medicine have uncovered the secret to the link between fish and heart disease: it's the type of fat in certain types of fish that confers the health benefits. This is called omega-3 fat, and today we know that it can benefit our heart health in a whole range of ways, including:

- Decreasing the risk of death from a heart attack among people who have not been diagnosed with heart disease
- Decreasing the risk of death among people who have had a previous heart attack
- Preventing potentially dangerous abnormal rhythms in the heart
- Lowering blood pressure

Groundbreaking news from the American Heart Association was released in November 2002 when this official organization of heart doctors urged all Americans to eat more healthy fat from fish and plants to help protect their hearts. Yes, you may have heard this advice before. So ... what's the *groundbreaking* part of the news? It's that, for the very first time, the American Heart Association made official recommendations about *how much* of these fish fats you should eat. If you don't have heart disease, they recommend enjoying at least two fish meals weekly, and mostly choosing fatty fish such as salmon, mackerel, and tuna. There are also specific guidelines for people who do have heart disease or high triglycerides (a type of fat in the blood that can increase the risk of heart disease, somewhat similarly to cholesterol). You'll read more about these guidelines, and how to meet them, in Chapter 2: The Power of Omega-3 in Heart Disease.

To further increase your appetite for our delicious recipes such as Garlic Roasted Salmon and Ginger Seared Tuna (see Chapter 8), the omega-3 fats the fish contain can benefit our body and even our mind in a myriad of other ways. These are just some of the ways scientists think omega-3s may help us to achieve optimal health:

- Reducing the immune system's attack on the body in such diseases as:
    Rheumatoid arthritis
    Systemic lupus erythematosus (often called lupus or SLE)
    Psoriasis
    Asthma
    Ulcerative colitis
- Decreasing blood clotting factors, which not only helps decrease heart attack risk, but also stroke risk
- Preventing or slowing the leading cause of blindness, macular degeneration
- Reducing the growth of certain types of cancer cells
- Alleviating and/or preventing certain types of depression and mental illness
- Improving the health of people with type 2 diabetes
- Curbing the frequency or severity of migraine headaches
- Helping fetal brains, nervous systems, and eyes develop normally, and . . .
- . . . Once babies are born, helping them grow and develop normally, especially their eyes and brains

One More Reason to Eat More Omega-3s . . .

Even if you don't have any of the conditions noted above (and even if you aren't having a baby), you should still worry about getting more healthy omega-3s from fish in your diet for one special reason: you might be deficient in this *essential fat*. Yes, omega-3 fats are an essential nutrient, which means that our bodies need them to function at optimal health, but we cannot make them ourselves. Thus, we must rely on getting them from food.

A worrying fact is that even if you're not interested in eating foods high in omega-3 to prevent disease or help a health condition you already have, research shows that you'd better start soon—as many Americans are not getting enough omega-3 fats to satisfy the body's basic everyday needs. To highlight this important point, a May 2002 press release from the American Dietetic Association, just prior to Mother's Day, announced that a low intake of omega-3 fats is one of the leading nutrition concerns for women in their "mom years." And moms are not the only people missing out. Studies have shown that some Americans are consuming just 20% of the recommended amounts of the essential omega-3 fats.

So why do we need omega-3 fats for everyday good health? Adults and children alike must have sufficient omega-3 fats in their diet for healthy:

- Skin
- Brain cells
- Eye tissue and vision

Babies are especially sensitive to not getting enough essential fat; those who are fed a skim-milk formula (*note that this is* **not** *recommended*) low in essential fats are at risk of:

- Not growing properly
- Trouble with hair growth
- Scaly skin

But Do I Have to Eat Fish?

The American Heart Association's influential new report answers this question—with major caveats. While there is a type of omega-3 fat found in plants such as walnuts and flaxseed, and some studies have found that it provides some protection against heart disease, this fat does not bring the same wide range of health benefits as the omega-3s found in fish. Our bodies have the ability to convert or transform the plant omega-3 to the much more beneficial types found in fish, but scientific studies have shown that little of the plant omega-3 we eat actually does get converted. Our bodies simply are not very efficient in doing this. With that explanation, you can understand the answers posed in the question "Do I have to eat fish?":

- If you don't have high triglycerides, you *may* be able to eat enough of the plant-type of omega-3 fat to meet your requirements for the type of omega-3s found in fish—you will need to be very diligent in eating plant sources of omega-3s.
- If you have high triglycerides, you will not be able to get enough fish-type omega-3s from plant foods. Instead, speak to your physician about whether or not you should take fish oil capsules (*don't* do this without speaking to your physician, as there are potentially dangerous side-effects, including excessive bleeding). As mentioned above, there are health benefits in eating the plant-based omega-3 fats, so please do include foods rich in them regularly in your diet even if you are taking fish oil capsules.

Later in this book, you'll learn more about the following foods; these supply the highest amount of plant-based omega 3s, and are the foods that non-fish eaters will need to eat regularly to maximize their body's levels of the fish-type omega-3s:

- Walnut oil and walnuts
- Canola oil
- Arugula (a salad green) and some other greens
- Soy products, such as tofu, soybeans, soymilk, and tempeh
- Flaxseed and flaxseed oil

This Book Will Help You to Understand:

- How scientists discovered the dramatic health benefits of omega-3 fats and why they can improve our health in such a myriad of ways, which fish have the most, and the best ways to cook fish to reel in the best catch of heart-healthy fats (Chapter 1)
- How fish fats work their wonders in preventing heart disease (Chapter 2)
- The surprising ways fish fats prevent or relieve many other health conditions (Chapter 3)
- What foods are rich in omega-3 fats, and what to do if you aren't able to eat enough of the most valuable fish-type omega-3s (Chapter 4)
- How to buy, store, and *easy ways* to cook fish (Chapter 5)
- How to buy, store, and use sources of plant omega-3s (Chapter 6)
- A perspective on how omega-3s fit into your life—in other words, the whole picture of a healthy lifestyle (Chapter 7)
- Mouth-watering recipes high in the healthy fish fats as well as plant-based omega-3s (Chapter 8)

In addition, I will provide you with 4 weeks of meal plans—in two sets of menus:

- One four-week set for people who like fish
- One four-week set for people who do not want to eat fish

Omega-3s to My Rescue— in Six Life-Saving Ways

I have a very special interest in the healthy fish fats (and also the plant sources of omega-3 fats). I believe, in fact, that they continually save my life. This is because I live daily with:

- Systemic lupus erythematosus
- Asthma
- Psoriasis and psoriatic arthritis

- High cholesterol, triglycerides, and hypertension
- Type 2 diabetes
- Migraines

But I live well with all of these diseases because of the way I eat (and the other lifestyle choices I make). You may be picturing me in a wheelchair, or perhaps sitting around trying to catch my breath, or aching in pain. Erase that thought! Now, I work full time as a chef, registered dietitian, and an author; I garden (and garden, and garden some more!), exercise 30 to 60 minutes daily, and enjoy hobbies and activities with my family. Today, my blood pressure averages 123/73, and my blood cholesterol/blood fat levels are:

- Total cholesterol: 174
- LDL-cholesterol (the bad one): 78 (you read correctly— seventy-eight)
- HDL-cholesterol (the good one): 81 (again, you read correctly)
- Triglycerides (fasting): 98

Compare this to just three years ago—when I was just 43—and my levels came in at:

- Total cholesterol: 228
- LDL-cholesterol: 129
- HDL-cholesterol: 49
- Triglycerides (fasting): 221

As you can imagine, I was in big trouble—from just my blood cholesterol levels alone! Add to that the lupus, the asthma, the type 2 diabetes, and the psoriasis/psoriatic arthritis. I was hurting—and afraid that I was a heart attack waiting to happen.

It was clear that I had to make some changes in my life—quickly. As a registered dietitian, I thought I was doing a pretty good job already! In fact, I didn't even think that I could tweak my diet any further. I had cut out red meat; I ate small amounts of skinless chicken and turkey breasts, loads of wholegrain foods, legumes, and a rainbow of fruits and vegetables daily.

Fish Fats Swim to My Rescue

I knew it was time to start studying, time to start learning what I could do better. That is when I learned more about fish fats and the plant sources of omega-3 fats. And that's when my health started turning around.

Indeed, today I am much healthier, and my life is rich and full. A dear friend once told me that the best way to live a good and healthy life is to get a chronic disease and learn to take care of it. Eating a diet that includes foods rich in omega-3 fats is one key part of my permanent life-giving, life-enhancing health plan. I'll tell you more about the *total* lifestyle picture in Chapter 7: A Perspective on Omega-3s: The Whole Picture of a Healthy Lifestyle! But first, in Chapter 1, I'll help you understand those valuable omega-3 fats and how scientists discovered their benefits.

Chapter 1

The Omega-3 Story: What Are Omega-3s? How Did We Discover Their Health Benefits?

It all Began with a Tall Fish Tale

The omega-3 story starts with a mystery. Danish scientists were studying a group of Eskimos living their traditional lifestyle in the frigid Arctic north of Greenland in the early 1970s. The scientists were trying to make sense of what seemed like a scientific impossibility—the Eskimos were eating a diet that contained a massive 40% fat and sky-high amounts of cholesterol, yet they were almost *heart attack free*. In addition, in spite of the huge amounts of fat (33% more than is generally recommended as healthy today, and mostly from animals, not vegetable oils) and cholesterol in their diet, the level of cholesterol in their blood was not particularly high.

These findings didn't even seem possible. Common knowledge said that eating a lot of animal fat and cholesterol should be literally killing the Eskimos.

The research team went to work to unravel this mystery. They first checked into inheritance—could the Eskimos be fortunate enough to have good genes that protected them from heart disease, no matter what they ate? But this theory did not pan out. The scientists found that not all Eskimos in Greenland had such low heart-attack rates. In fact, Eskimos eating a less traditional diet had much higher rates of heart disease, and those Eskimos who lived in Denmark and were eating a typical Danish diet had roughly the same rates of heart disease as the Danes. It seemed that it must be something in the traditional diet that was the heart-protective factor.

Researchers compared the food intake of Eskimos who ate a very traditional diet, almost solely composed of fish and seal meat and blubber, with some walrus and whale thrown in for variety, with those who ate less traditionally or ate a typical Danish diet. They found a striking difference. The primary sources of animal fat in the Eskimos' traditional diet are fish, seal, walrus, and whales. While the latter three are officially considered animals, they are not land animals, but instead *marine* animals, or animals that live in the sea. Marine animal fat differs significantly from that of land animals such as cows, pigs, or sheep. Land animal fat was the primary source of fat in the less traditional diets; this type of fat is largely saturated fat, the type that tends to raise blood cholesterol levels, a risk factor for heart disease. Marine animals and fish both contain a special type of fat called omega-3 fat, which we now know has many benefits to our health, especially heart health. Therein lies the secret to why the Eskimos, when eating their native diet, had virtually no heart disease. Such a minor difference, one would think, but it contributes to such major effects on health.

Eskimo Diets: The Fishy Facts

Traditional Eskimo diet:

+ Fish, fish, and more fish
+ Lots of walrus, whale, and seal
- Hardly any cheese, butter, or whole milk
- Little meat from land-based animals
= LITTLE fat from land-based animals
= LOTS and LOTS of fat from fish and marine animals

Less traditional Eskimo diet:

- Less fish
- Less walrus, whale, and seal
+ Much, much more cheese, butter, and whole milk
+ Much more meat from land-based animals
= TOO MUCH fat from land-based animals
= TOO LITTLE fat from fish and marine animals

Indeed, Greenland's Eskimos were not the only people to teach us about the importance of fish in a naturally heart-healthy diet. Scientists were also fascinated by their findings when they studied the diet and health of men in a small seaside village in rural Japan. Although the Japanese villagers ate quite large amounts of fish, in contrast to the Eskimos, they ate a very low-fat diet overall. As we might expect, they tended to be slim and have low cholesterol levels. We might also expect them to have a low incidence of heart disease. However, scientists found the Japanese villagers' rate of heart disease was exceedingly low. In fact, their rate of death from any cause at all was much lower than it would have been in an equivalent group of men in the United States.

As with the Eskimos, the researchers have concluded that the Japanese men's exceptional health was directly linked to their high fish intake, and to the very valuable fats the fish contain: the omega-3 fats.

What's in a Name?

You might also see omega-3 fats called by the following names—all of which are correct:

- ► omega-3 fatty acids
- ► n-3 fats or n-3 fatty acids
- ► ω-3 fats (ω is the Greek symbol for omega)
- ► n-3 PUFAS, where PUFA stands for polyunsaturated fatty acids
- ► omega-3 fats

For simplicity's sake, I'll call them omega-3 fats or omega-3s throughout this book.

Just What Are Omega-3 Fats ?

Omega-3 fats are polyunsaturated fats. What does this mean? Well you've probably heard that there are three main types of fats Mother Nature makes:

- Saturated fats (the most villainous of fats in terms of raising blood cholesterol levels and clogging the arteries)
- Polyunsaturated fats
- Monounsaturated fats

You may have also seen these words on food packaging, such as on margarine containers. As a first step in understanding omega-3s, I will demystify these terms. All types of fat are made of building blocks. The building blocks are hooked or "bonded" together. For the sake of simplicity, think of the bonds as paper clips. In saturated fats, all the bonds are single bonds, or single paper clips. In polyunsaturated or monounsaturated fats, the building blocks may be hooked together with double bonds—the equivalent of two paper clips.

So what about "poly-" versus "mono-" unsaturated fats? "Monos" is the Greek term for single, or one, while "polus" is the Greek term for many. As you might have guessed by now, monounsaturated fats have just one double (or two paper clip) bond. Polyunsaturated fats, such as omega-3 fats, have two or more of these double paper-clip bonds.

In naming mono- and polyunsaturated fats, scientists count back from the end with the last building block tacked on—called the omega end—to find the first double bond. In omega-3s, the first double bond occurs three building blocks away from the omega end. And there we've uncovered the mystery behind how omega-3s got their name.

We'll talk more about the different types of fat and their effects on our health, particularly our cholesterol levels, in the next chapter; for now I want to concentrate on the omega-3s. There are three main omega-3 fats, which I've grouped into two categories: those found in fish and those found in plant foods:

Omega-3s found in fish:

- *Eicosapentaenoic* (pronounced: i-KO'sa-pen-ten-O'ik) *acid* (usually called EPA)—found in seafood, especially cold-water fish.
- *Docosahexaenoic* (pronounced: do-KO'sa-hecks-en-O'ik) *acid* (usually called DHA)—also found in seafood, especially cold-water fish.

Omega-3s found in plant foods:

- *Alpha-linolenic* (pronounced: lino-LEN'ik) *acid* (often called ALA)—found in flaxseed, tofu and other soybean products, canola oil, walnuts, arugula, and other greens.

It's always a mystery, even to me as a nutrition and food expert, why certain foods contain particular nutrients and kinds of fat. I guess that is Mother Nature's decision to make! We do know a little about why some fish have more omega-3s than others do. Fish scientists have discovered that omega-3 is just fish "body fat," which helps fish adapt to the cold water in which they live, just as human body fat insulates us from the cold. So it's no coincidence that many of the fish containing the highest amounts of this valuable fat, such as salmon and herring, tend to come from the most frigid seas and oceans. To make omega-3s, fish living in these deep cold waters eat a tiny sea plant called phytoplankton (found most abundantly in deep waters). Researchers have found, in fact, that the amount of omega-3s normally occurring in cold-water fish decrease substantially if they are not present in the food consumed by the fish. In sum, think of omega-3s as the insulation layer for cold-water fish.

Here's one more important fact about omega-3s, and how the three types listed above relate to each other. When you eat omega-3s from plant foods, the body converts a little of the alpha-linolenic acid or ALA to the two types of omega-3s found in fish, eicosapentaenoic acid (EPA for short) and docosahexaenoic acid (DHA). Remember this point, as it will take on a great significance for those of you who don't eat fish as we broaden our understanding of omega-3s and their health benefits.

Two Essential Fats: Omega-3s and Omega-6s

I mentioned above that omega-3s are one of the polyunsaturated fats. There is one other main type of polyunsaturated fat, the omega-6 fats. From what you've learned about the structure and naming of fats, you'll be correct in thinking that this type of fat has its first double bond occurring six building blocks away from the omega end.

Together, these two types of fat, the omega-3s and omega-6s, form the essential fats. In other words, like vitamins and minerals, they are a necessary part of our diet and enable our bodies to function at optimal health. It may seem surprising that there are fats that are essential to our health, particularly as we are always hearing health experts telling us to cut down our fat intake. The fact is that some fats, particularly the saturated fats, are harmful to us, especially when eaten in large amounts. Other fats have more healthful qualities, and others, the polyunsaturated omega-3s and omega-6s, are essential to us at all ages and stages of our life. Again like the vitamins and minerals, we don't require very large amounts of these fats for good health—we'll learn more about exactly how much we need of the essential fats later (and how to cut down on the harmful ones). For now, just note that, in the appropriate amounts, essential fats have key roles to play in our bodies. These include:

- Regulating the "traffic" of substances and fluids in and out of all cells in the body
- Maintaining healthy hair
- Regulating cholesterol metabolism
- Helping form hormones
- Guarding and maintaining the health of the reproductive system
- Keeping the immune system healthy

Omega-3s and omega-6s: The differences

So what's the difference between omega-3s and omega-6s? In a physical sense, the most basic contrast is that the first double bond (or double paper clip) is in a slightly altered place. Yes, it's a very small distinction, but you'll see that it can make a world of difference to our health.

The second difference is in where you find these essential fats. As you read earlier, the omega-3 fats are found mainly in fish and other seafood, and plant sources such as flaxseed, soybean products, canola oil, and walnuts. The omega-6 fats tend to come from foods that are more common in our diets, including most vegetable oils and most nuts and seeds.

- Omega-3s include *alpha-linolenic* acid (ALA) from plant sources, also eicosapentaenoic acid (EPA) and docosahexaenoic acid (DHA) from fish and other seafood.
- Omega-6s include *linoleic* acid (more simply called LA) from plant sources such as vegetable oils, margarines, seeds, and nuts. You might also see arachidonic acid (also called AA) listed when you read about omega-6 essential fats. While the body cannot make linoleic acid from other nutrients you eat, it does make arachidonic acid from the linoleic acid in your diet. Small amounts of arachidonic acid are also found in some lean meats, especially game, and eggs, however most of it is made by the body from the linoleic acid you eat.

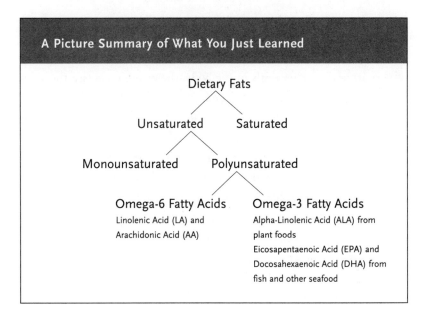

A Picture Summary of What You Just Learned

Dietary Fats

Unsaturated   Saturated

Monounsaturated   Polyunsaturated

Omega-6 Fatty Acids
Linolenic Acid (LA) and
Arachidonic Acid (AA)

Omega-3 Fatty Acids
Alpha-Linolenic Acid (ALA) from
plant foods
Eicosapentaenoic Acid (EPA) and
Docosahexaenoic Acid (DHA) from
fish and other seafood

The other main difference is that omega-3s and omega-6s, though very closely related, are individual types of essential fat with distinct health effects in the body. Omega-3s have certain crucial roles in the body that omega-6s do not. Remember those fish fats we talked about—EPA and DHA—which the body can also make if you eat enough omega-3s from plant sources? These fats have very special functions in the body—they are the ones needed in the most active energy-exchanging and oxygen-requiring tissues, such as:

- Brain
- Retina of the eye
- Adrenal gland
- Testicular tissues

This means the fish-based omega-3s are particularly important during pregnancy and for infants, when the baby's nervous system, brain, and eyes are developing.

Omega-3s and omega-6s: Working together for health

It's easy to see why both omega-3s and omega-6s are essential to our health, but how do omega-3s benefit our bodies in so many ways, from combatting heart disease to easing the pain of arthritis. The key to many positive effects of omega-3 fats lie in their influence on a group of very important chemicals in the body, the eicosanoids (see the sidebar on page 10 for a more detailed explanation of these chemicals). Both omega-3 and omega-6 fats produce the same eicosanoid chemicals, but those derived from omega-6s tend to promote blood clotting, artery constriction, and inflammation. These are all important and necessary body processes; after all, if our blood didn't clot we would bleed to death from a little cut. However, too much of these omega-6 effects can cause problems, such as increased blood pressure or the inflammation that accompanies rheumatoid arthritis.

In contrast, the eicosanoid chemicals produced from the omega-3 fats are said to be more 'soothing,' and tend to reduce inflammation, allow our arteries to relax, and make blood less likely to clot. From this, you can see that our health could benefit from having more omega-3 fats in our diet rather than more omega-6s, though we know we need both types as they are both essential to our health in many ways. This is exactly what health experts, including the American Heart Association, are telling us—eat more omega-3 fats. As you can imagine, it is also thought that the ratio of omega-3s to omega-6s in our diet is likely to be important; in other words, we probably need to eat enough omega-3s to keep their artery-relaxing, anti-inflammatory effects in balance with the opposite effects of the omega-6s. This idea is controversial, but some scientists think that this ratio may be critical to our health and well-being.

To try to decide what ratio or balance we should be eating, scientists have looked at the diets of people in the world, such as the Japanese villagers we discussed earlier, whose health and hearts have benefitted from the fish they eat. The general Japanese population is well known for their love of fish, and they consume an average of four times as many omega-6 fats as omega-3s. Researchers have also looked at the diets of our ancestors from Paleolithic times, and found that their diet supplied them with between one and four times as much omega-6 as omega-3 fat. The best advice, then, is to eat no more than four times as much omega-6 as omega-3. We learned this also from the famous Lyon Heart Study, which studied diets followed by 605 people and showed that eating like this decreases the risk of sudden death from heart disease.

While this might sound like you'll need to increase your omega-6s, nothing could be further from the truth. In fact, most Americans eat far more than four times the amount of omega-6s as omega-3s—generally about ten times and sometimes as much as 100 times! When you see this, it seems very clear—we must dramatically increase our intake of the essential omega-3 fats to ensure optimal health.

The Eicosanoids: Following the Omega-3 Path to Better Health

A major way the omega-3s improve our health is by their influence on the eicosanoid chemicals, a group of naturally occurring body chemicals that have wide ranging effects in our bodies. Among their many effects, the eicosanoids produced from omega-6 fats, including most vegetable oils and margarines, tend to raise blood pressure and promote immune reactions and inflammation. Those produced from omega-3 fats, the fish oils, have the opposite effect, calming the immune system and reducing blood pressure and inflammation. Let's take a closer look at a few of the main eicosanoid chemicals. Each of these may be produced from either omega-3 or omega-6 fats, and this will influence their action in the body.

- ► Prostaglandins: Substances found in many tissues, with a variety of effects on these tissues, including:
  - Vasoconstriction, or causing blood vessels to contract or squeeze together
  - Vasodilation, or causing blood vessels to relax
  - Stimulation of intestinal muscle, which causes it to contract and speed waste through the body
  - Stimulation of the bronchial, or lung, tissue, which helps breathing and coughing, and getting rid of phlegm in the lungs
  - Uterine stimulation, which is a help in childbirth

- ► Leukotrienes
  - One of the gatekeepers, or controllers, of the amount of inflammation in the body
  - Play a role in allergic reactions

(continued on next page)

► Thromboxanes
  • Affect the platelets, the disc-shaped cells in the blood that help blood clot; we need platelets to stop us from bleeding when we get a cut; platelets also limit the amount of bruising we get under our skin after a bump.

The body needs a balance of these chemicals derived from omega-3s and omega-6s to function normally, and too-high concentrations of eicosanoids produced from omega-6 fats may lead to increased inflammation associated with several conditions, including arthritis and asthma. While just the right balance causes the blood vessels to contract and relax appropriately to control blood pressure, an imbalance may really put the squeeze on blood vessels and result in higher blood pressure. It could also encourage platelets—one of the clotting substances in blood that keeps us from bleeding excessively—to clump overtime, and therefore clog up arteries. You'll read more about each of these processes in Chapters 2 and 3.

How Much Omega-3 Does My Body Need?

It's absolutely clear that almost all of us don't have enough omega-3s in our diet. In addition, most of us probably aren't eating enough omega-3s to balance the effects of the omega-6 fats that are much more common in our diet. Thus, in discussing how much omega-3 fat you need, it's important to think about two main points:

1) How much omega-3 fat you need in your diet
2) The amount of omega-3s you eat daily compared to omega-6s—called the ratio

For many people, there will be another very important question to consider:

3) What to do if you don't eat fish

How much omega-3 do I need?

Of these three points, the easy one is how much omega-3 you should take in each week. The American Heart Association's new guidelines, issued in November 2002, recommend that people who do not have heart disease have at least two fish meals weekly. They should eat a variety of fish, with an emphasis on choosing those highest in the beneficial fish fats, the EPA and DHA. Best choices therefore include salmon, mackerel, tuna, and sardines. The American Heart Association also recommends that people increase their consumption of the plant sources of omega-3s by eating more of the foods highest in alpha-linolenic acid or ALA. These include flaxseed, walnuts, canola and soybean oil.

There are different guidelines for people who have been diagnosed with heart disease and those with high levels of triglycerides, a substance your doctor may test for when checking your cholesterol levels. We'll look at these guidelines in Chapter 2, The Power of Omega-3 in Heart Disease. Chapter 4 will help you to choose the best food sources of both fish and plant omega-3s, and look no further than Chapters 5 and 6 for practical advice and cooking tips for all of these heart healthy super-foods.

Striking a balance: omega-3s and omega-6s

The more difficult point concerns the ratio of omega-3s to omega-6s. Although there is a seemingly small physical difference between omega-3s and omega-6s—just in where the first double bond (those double paper clips) falls—the main difference is how they act in the body, as you've read above. For example, while omega-3s seem to protect against the inflammation of rheumatoid arthritis, omega-6s—in excess—may promote this inflammation. One way to cut down on the effect of inflammatory substances formed from omega-6s is to eat more omega-3s. Another way to take your diet toward the healthy balance of omega-6s and omega-3s is to moderate your intake of the omega-6s. You'll recall that most of us are eating at least ten times as many omega-6s as omega-3s. The overall strategy, then, is to moderate your intake of omega-6s and increase your intake of omega-3s; this will take you towards the healthy 4:1 ratio.

How do you moderate your intake of omega-6s? The main sources of this type of polyunsaturated fat are very common in our diet: most vegetable oils, including sunflower, safflower, and corn oil, margarines made from these oils, and processed foods containing these vegetable oils. By reducing the amount of oil we use in cooking, cutting back on the spread on our bread, and watching our intake of processed foods, we reduce our intake of omega-6s. By also changing the type of oil and margarine to canola and soybean varieties, we get the added bonus of extra omega-3s.

We don't need to worry that cutting down our omega-6 intake will mean we don't get enough of this type of essential fat—we have much more than we need in our diet already. On the contrary, as well as helping our balance with omega-3 fats, reducing our intake of omega-6 fats may also benefit our health by helping us control our weight.

What if I don't eat fish?

We've talked a lot about the benefits of the omega-3s found in fish, and seen recommendations to eat fish several times a week, but how does this translate for those of you who don't eat fish? You may simply not like the taste of fish, or you may not be able to eat seafood due to a food allergy or intolerance. Does this mean you have to miss out on the health-giving properties of the omega-3s? The answer is no, but you will have to be a lot more diligent with your diet if you wish to reap their rewards.

The reason we've talked so much about the omega-3s found in fish and less about those from plant sources is because the fish fats have health benefits that the linolenic acid from the plant sources does not have. This is not to say that it does not have benefits; for example, scientific studies have clearly demonstrated that alpha-linolenic acid protects against heart disease—just not in as many ways as the fish-based omega-3s. As I explained earlier, some of the alpha-linolenic acid we eat does get converted into the much more beneficial types of omega-3s found in fish, but scientific studies have shown that it gets converted only in very small amounts. It may be as much as 15% or it may be much lower.

Given that no one is absolutely sure what the rate of conversion from plant to animal sources is, it is impossible to give an exact answer to how much of the plant omega-3s you'll need to eat for full protection. However, a good level to aim for, if you don't have heart disease and don't eat fish, is at least 3 to 4 grams per day of omega-3s from plant sources; this is likely to be close to the equivalent of two oily fish meals a week. You'll find a lot more information on what you will need to eat to achieve this in Chapter 4. That chapter will also discuss the omega-3-enriched eggs you may have seen in your supermarket, and whether they might be suitable for you if you don't eat fish. If you have heart disease or high triglyceride levels, you will need to look at Chapter 2 first to see the specific recommendations that apply to you. Be warned that it will require an exceptionally careful diet to fight established heart disease through omega-3s if you don't eat fish, and recommended omega-3 intakes to lower high triglyceride levels are even larger. Fish-oil supplements may be the answer for some people—later chapters will answer all your questions.

While we've always talked of fish as brain food (and now we know how important it is to the development of tiny babies' brains), it is only recently that we've realized it is also healthy heart food, arthritic joint food, good mood food, and so much more. In the following chapters we'll explore the many, many ways omega-3s can improve the health of men and women, older adults, and developing babies. Then, in Chapter 4, I'll show you the very best sources of these valuable nutrients.

Chapter 2

The Power of Omega-3 in Heart Disease

Not eating fish may be detrimental to your heart. Evidence is compelling, consistent, and persistent from around the world that fish eaters are less likely to get and die from heart disease than people who do not eat fish. More good news is that scientists have found that we don't need to eat as much fish as the Eskimos we learned about in Chapter 1 (or any of the walrus or seals they ate!); just a few fish meals each week can bring us better heart health. And today—fortunately for people who do not like fish—we also know that people can reap some of the benefits of the omega-3s from other food sources such as walnuts and linseeds.

One study found that eating an average of just over one ounce or more of fish daily (only about eight ounces weekly, or two regular-sized portions):

- Reduced men's risk of death from heart disease by nearly 40% (to be exact, 38%)
- Slashed men's risk of having a heart attack by nearly 60%

Harvard researchers (studying over 20,000 male physicians) discovered that eating just one omega-3 rich fish meal each week:

- Lowered the risk of sudden cardiac death (when the heart stops beating) by 52%

And a major study of female nurses reported that women who ate fish just once a week:

- Reduced their risk of death from heart disease by 29%

Blood pressure experts say that if you have normal blood pressure, eating fish three to four times per week may reduce your risk of developing high blood pressure; if you already have high blood pressure, eating fish can help lower your readings.

Before taking a look at how omega-3 fats help fight heart disease—and even give hope to those who already have it—I would like to walk you through some of the basic principles of this very common and frequently life-threatening problem. You'll see how our diet, particularly the type of fat we eat, relates to cholesterol levels and heart disease, and the process by which our arteries actually become blocked. This heart disease primer will be a big help in understanding how omega-3s swim to the rescue.

Diet and Heart Disease—a Primer

There are many factors in our health and diet that can make us more or less likely to develop heart disease, and therefore influence our risk of having a heart attack. Unfortunately, some of these are things we can't change. For example, we are more likely to suffer from heart disease if we have a family history of this health problem, in other words if we know that our parents or other close relatives have or had heart disease or heart attacks. Other "risk factors" we cannot change include our age and being male (we are more likely to develop heart disease as we get older or if we are male). The positive side to this is that there are many other factors we can influence, such as our weight, blood pressure, and cholesterol levels, simply by eating healthily and exercising regularly. You can read more about an overall healthy diet for your heart in Chapter 7, but here we'll discuss the effect of fat and other areas of our diet on our levels of cholesterol and a similar compound, triglyceride, in our blood.

Most of us know that certain types of fat are bad for our health or, more specifically, bad for our heart. You may have heard your doctor tell you to eat less saturated fat, or seen labels boasting that a cooking oil or margarine is high in monounsaturated fat. In the last chapter we looked at the differences in the physical makeup of these types of fat. You'll remember that there were no double bonds (or double paper clips) between the building blocks of the saturated fats, just one double bond in the monounsaturated fats, and two or more double paper-clip bonds in the polyunsaturated fats (which include the omega-3s and the omega-6s). While this seems like a very small difference, it can have a very large impact on our cholesterol levels.

Understanding cholesterol

Whether you have heart disease or are trying to prevent it, you are probably concerned about your cholesterol reading and what you can do to make it healthier. Let's back up, though, and get a good grip on this slippery substance called cholesterol.

The term cholesterol tends to conjure up only negative thoughts. However, everyone needs cholesterol to live. It is a waxy substance found in our blood and is an essential ingredient in many natural and normal body substances, including skin oils, hormones, and digestive juices. It is so necessary to good health that the body actually makes cholesterol in the liver. Problems only start to occur when our cholesterol level becomes too high—you can check your cholesterol levels against the ideal levels in the *Know Your Cholesterol—and Other Important Numbers* sidebar in this chapter.

Before talking more about cholesterol, it's important to distinguish between cholesterol in the blood and cholesterol in food. When doctors tell us to watch our cholesterol levels, they are referring to the level of cholesterol in our blood. It's natural to assume that all the cholesterol in our blood comes from the cholesterol we eat in food, but this is definitely not the case. In fact, the vast majority of the cholesterol in our blood is made by our own body in our liver. The main building block for the cholesterol our body makes is the saturated fat (mostly from animal fats and processed foods) in our diet. This is the first part of the puzzle of how the fat in our diet influences our cholesterol levels.

All cholesterol is not created equal

Cholesterol is carried around from one part of the body to another via the bloodstream. Just as oil or wax will not dissolve in water, waxy cholesterol by itself cannot dissolve in blood. To overcome this transportation problem, the liver sends the cholesterol around the body in small packages. The way cholesterol is packaged plays a more critical role than just moving cholesterol particles through the blood: it determines how cholesterol impacts the health of the blood vessels through which it travels, and ultimately the heart. Although the packages all contain cholesterol, they have quite different, sometimes opposite, effects on heart disease. You may have heard the names LDL, low density lipoproteins, and HDL, high density lipoproteins, if you've had your cholesterol levels tested; doctors often check these to get a more complete picture of your heart disease risk. These are two of the main types of cholesterol package.

LDL is often called the "bad" cholesterol as high levels raise our risk of heart disease. With their high content of cholesterol and triglycerides (read more about triglycerides below), LDL particles are more likely to lodge in our arteries, contributing to atherosclerosis or hardening of the arteries. Conversely, HDL is frequently termed the "good" cholesterol because it protects us against heart disease. Think of HDL particles as the good guys who come to the rescue to move cholesterol and other fats out of the bloodstream to be removed from the body. There's one more type of cholesterol to consider: VLDL, very low density lipoproteins. You probably haven't heard much discussion of VLDL-cholesterol, mostly because it doesn't hang around in the bloodstream very long. Nevertheless, it may be sinister, as VLDL particles contain large amounts of cholesterol and triglycerides, and have great potential to adhere to the arteries and contribute to blockages.

As you can see, there's a lot more to cholesterol than just the total amount in our blood. Knowing that LDLs are bad and HDLs good, it's easy to understand that heart troubles can arise when too much cholesterol gets packaged as LDL particles. This also helps us appreciate why we need to know more than just our total cholesterol level. What influences the types of cholesterol we have in our blood? Well, some of this certainly is determined by our genetics (which is one reason that our family history tells us about our risk of heart disease, as I mentioned earlier), but the type of fat we eat certainly plays a major role.

Know Your Fats

With fat in so many places in our diet, and quite a few different types of fat to be found, it can get a bit confusing. Here's a useful guide to knowing what fat is on your plate; just read down each column to check where the different types of fat come from in your diet. To make the situation more complex, you'll see that some oils, such as olive oil, are in two different lists. Look at the *Another Note on Fats* sidebar to find out why.

Polyunsaturated fat—omega-3	Polyunsaturated fat—omega-6	Monounsaturated fat	Saturated fat
Fish	Sunflower oil	Olive oil and olives	Fat from meats, eg. lard or
Shellfish	Safflower oil	Canola oil	the fat on a steak
Flaxseed and oil	Corn oil	Peanut oil	Fat from dairy foods, eg. cream
Walnuts and walnut oil	Soybean oil	Avocados	and butter
Canola oil	Margarines made with	Margarines made with	Palm oil
Soybean oil and soy-based	omega-6 oils	monounsaturated oils	Coconut oil
foods, eg. tofu	Foods made with omega-6 oils	Foods made with	Foods made from saturated
Margarines made with	Some seeds, eg. sunflower and	monounsaturated oils	fats, including many
omega-6 oils	sesame seeds	Most nuts, eg. macadamia nuts	processed foods, such as
Foods made with omega-3 oils		and their oil, almonds, and	some cookies and pastries
		pecans	and many fast foods
			Fatty meats, eg. bacon and
			sausages

Those small changes in the physical structure of fats discussed in Chapter 1 influence our heart health via the type of cholesterol that travels around in our bloodstream. I told you earlier that saturated fat, the one with no double bonds, tends to increase our LDL-cholesterol levels. It compounds the problem by pushing down our levels of the good HDL-cholesterol. Saturated fats are found in animal foods, such as the fat in dairy foods and meat, and in many processed foods such as cakes and cookies. (There's another villainous type of fat, called trans fat, that acts in a similar way to saturated fat. You can read more about it in Chapter 7.)

On the other hand, by substituting the monounsaturated fats (the ones with one double bond) for saturated fats, we can lower LDL levels

Another Note on Fats

Note one more, somewhat confusing, point about all foods that contain fat: any food that contains fat has all three types of fat (saturated, monounsaturated, and polyunsaturated). Because one type of fat predominates, a food is generally referred to by that type. In other words, the fat in a food generally is called by the name of the predominating fat. Olive oil, for example, is deemed a "monounsaturated" fat because 75 percent of the fat in it is monounsaturated. However, it also contains some polyunsaturated and a little saturated fat. Even butter, which consists of 62% saturated fat, contains 30% monounsaturated fats.

Fats that are predominantly poly- and monounsaturated are liquid at room temperature. Saturated fats are solid. Picture a bottle of liquid olive oil versus a stick of butter at room temperature, or the white waxy layer of saturated fat on a platter of cooling roast beef. And then realize that these saturated fats literally paint quite the same picture inside your arteries.

(continued on next page)

As a rule, fats of plant origin, such as vegetable oils, are almost entirely poly- and monounsaturated (the only two exceptions are coconut and palm oil, which are predominantly saturated fat and often found in processed foods). Animal fats—those in dairy foods, beef, pork, and chicken—are mostly saturated fat.

I'm going to put omega-3s, from both fish and plant sources, in an entirely different category because they have some unique benefits to human health.

without lowering our levels of the beneficial HDL-cholesterol. These monounsaturated fats are the predominant type in olive and canola oils, and their heart-healthy effect on cholesterol is one of the reasons we often see a Mediterranean diet, with its emphasis on olive oil, recommended by health experts. The omega-6 polyunsaturated fats, the ones that are found in most vegetable oils and margarines, also tend to lower the dangerous LDL-cholesterol; however, at the same time, they lower the amount of healthy HDL-cholesterol in our blood. The omega-3s, whether from fish or plant sources, can raise beneficial HDL levels slightly, but they don't have a very strong effect on cholesterol levels (although they have so many other beneficial effects on our heart health). In very large amounts, which would only occur if supplements were taken, omega-3s can actually increase LDL-cholesterol levels a little in susceptible people.

Understanding Triglycerides

Our triglyceride level is another thing the doctor might test when our cholesterol levels are checked. It's also another important way our diet and, in this case, our omega-3 intake can influence our risk of heart disease. Triglyceride is another form in which fat circulates in the blood; it's a little like cholesterol in this respect, and in the fact that levels that are too high can increase our risk of heart disease.

If we eat excess calories from any source—whether it is carbohydrates, protein, or fat—our bodies make triglycerides. When we really overeat, the excess amounts circulate in the bloodstream until they are stored as fat. In addition to overeating any type of calorie, drinking alcohol can cause the liver to produce excessive amounts of triglycerides. Overall, the American Heart Association says, triglyceride blood levels may be more accurate in predicting heart attack risk than was previously recognized.

There's one more point I'd like to make regarding how our diet impacts on our cholesterol and triglyceride levels. Although the vast majority of us can control these levels by following a healthy diet, exercising regularly, and controlling our weight, there are some people whose genetic makeup causes their body to make more cholesterol or to have higher triglyceride levels than the rest of us. Your doctor will be able to tell you if this is the case, and, even with the best diet in the world, you may need medication to control your levels of cholesterol and triglycerides.

Painting a Picture of the Artery-Clogging Process

How do LDL-cholesterol and triglycerides circulating in the blood increase our risk of heart disease? To answer this question, let's look at a blow-by-blow description of the process by which arteries become blocked and increase your risk of heart attack (and stroke):

- The inside of a blood vessel free of artery-clogging heart disease looks like a hollow tube that is clean and smooth on the inside. This allows blood to pass through completely freely, supplying life-giving oxygen to all parts of the body.
- When LDL-cholesterol and triglycerides start accumulating in the bloodstream at high levels, it causes damage to the inside of the artery. Other causes of damage include smoking and high blood pressure. The damaged cells inside the artery attract a sludge of substances, including LDL-cholesterol, platelets (a type of blood cell, you'll read more about these later in this chapter),

and calcium, to come out of the blood and start being deposited on the walls of arteries. This is the starting point of what is officially known as "atherosclerosis," or coronary artery disease. Frighteningly, it is happening to younger and younger people eating our typical American diet, and has even been found in the arteries of children.

- Over time, this sludge (known as a "plaque") causes the inside of your arteries to become rough and narrowed, limiting the supply of oxygen-rich blood to your heart muscle. Like a partly blocked pipe, there is just less room for the blood to get through.

- Once the artery is narrowed by this plaque, it is prone to other potentially dangerous changes that make the problem worse. For example:

  Blood cells flock to the affected area, trying to heal the damage. While this is a normal, protective mechanism of the body, it isn't good in this case. These extra cells further thicken the lining of the artery, making it narrower so even less blood gets through.

  In response to the narrowed vessel, the body sends out extra amounts of a naturally occurring chemical called thromboxane (one of the eicosanoid chemicals you read about in the last chapter), which may make blood clot too much.

This sets up the picture for a heart attack or a stroke to occur. The resulting clots can break off and travel to a smaller blood vessel where they may cut off blood supply to a part of the heart or the brain completely—this is a heart attack or stroke. Clots can also cause blood vessel spasm, again reducing blood flow through the artery. In addition, if the artery-narrowing process continues unchecked, the artery can become totally blocked off, stopping all blood flow to an area of the heart or brain and again causing a heart attack or stroke.

It's frighteningly clear how dangerous the process of heart disease is. Let's now look at how omega-3 fats can help us in the fight against this all-too-common illness.

How Omega-3s Protect Your Heart

Overall, omega-3s work many wonders within the bloodstream to prevent heart attacks, strokes, and to lower blood pressure. As you've read, just the omega-3s from a few fish meals each week can dramatically reduce our risk of heart disease. Here are some of the many things they do behind the scenes—as long as you take in enough through what you eat each week (don't worry—I'm going to help you with this!).

Omega-3s have clot-stopping powers

You read above that one of the problems in heart disease occurs when cells called platelets stick to the inside of the artery, reducing the amount of blood that can pass through. If a blood clot forms and blocks these narrowed arteries in the heart or the brain, a heart attack or stroke can occur. Omega-3s work in the body to combat both of these processes.

The platelets are cells in our blood that reduce the amount we bleed if we cut ourselves: they stick together and block the wound so more blood cannot escape. Obviously this is crucial to our survival—without this protective mechanism of the body, we could bleed to death from just a small injury. But when the platelets clot overtime, they increase our risk of heart disease, heart attacks, and strokes. By reducing the tendency of platelets to clump together too much, omega-3s both reduce the chance that platelets will stick to the lining of arteries and also lower the chance that they will stick together to form a clot that can cause a heart attack or stroke. Much of this health benefit is related to one of the eicosanoid chemicals we looked at in the previous chapter. Thromboxane derived from omega-6 fats tends to make blood clot more by making platelets more "sticky." By eating more omega-3s rather than omega-6s, we shift the balance to make less of the "sticky" thromboxane and more of the omega-3 type of thromboxane that reduces platelet clotting. Thus, the omega-3s reduce our risk of heart attacks and strokes caused by blood clots.

Omega-3s, beneficial in reducing clotting, can have a downside if people consume very excessive amounts of these healthy fats (much

Know Your Cholesterol—and Other Important Numbers

It's up to you to know the numbers that describe your heart disease risk. The following numbers are the desirable laboratory values for reducing heart disease risk:

- ► Total cholesterol: should be less than 200 mg/dL
- ► LDL-cholesterol: should be less than 100 mg/dL
- ► HDL-cholesterol:
  Should be greater than 45 mg/dL for men
  Should be greater than 55 mg/dL for women
- ► Triglycerides: should be less than 200 mg/dL
- ► Fasting blood glucose: should be 65 mg/dL to 110 mg/dL*
- ► Hemoglobin A1C: should be 4.0 to 6.0%*
- ► Blood pressure: should be less than 120/80

* It's important to know about your blood sugars, too, when reducing heart disease risk. This is because having blood sugars that are too high (such as when you have type 2 diabetes that is not well controlled, or even pre-diabetes) is the one of the leading causes of heart disease.

more than anyone would eat in their normal diet). The Eskimos who ate massive amounts of omega-3s from fish and marine animals had a miniscule rate of heart disease, but they did suffer more from one type of stroke than people on less "fishy" diets. These were not the type of strokes caused by clots that we talked about earlier; the strokes were a different type caused by bleeding from a blood vessel in the brain. While experts like the American Heart Association say there is no risk of this happening just from eating plenty of fish (no one is likely to eat as much as the Eskimos), they do advise caution if taking large amounts of fish-oil supplements. We'll talk more about this in Chapter 4, but the most important thing is always to discuss these supplements with your doctor before taking them.

Omega-3s decrease the amount of two bad fats in the blood: Triglycerides and VLDL

High levels of triglycerides and VLDL-cholesterol are associated with increased risk for heart disease. Many studies have shown that an increased intake of omega-3s bring the benefit of reduced triglyceride levels, even in people whose levels are very high. To treat these high levels however, the amount of omega-3 required is greater and would necessitate a fish-oil supplement. (Remember that it is essential that you discuss this with your physician before taking one.) Otherwise, for general heart protection, simply follow the guidelines at the end of the chapter for people with or without heart disease. This will bring the added bonus of keeping the liver from making too much potentially dangerous VLDL.

Omega-3s keep down inflammation inside the arteries

In more recent years, heart experts have discovered that inflammation inside the arteries plays a role in them becoming blocked. In fact, the whole artery-clogging process is thought to begin with inflammation. Omega-3s put the brakes on this inflammation. Again, this is believed to be related to their influence on the eicosanoid chemicals discussed in the last chapter. By increasing omega-3s (and moderating omega-6s) we move the balance away from the "aggressive" eicosanoids that cause inflammation and toward the more "calming" anti-inflammatory versions of these chemicals. In turn, this reduces the amount of "plaque" that accumulates and sticks to the lining of the arteries.

Omega-3s protect the heart's electrical system, thereby reducing the risk of dangerous abnormal heartbeats

Although you don't realize it, your heart beats an average of 72 times each minute, or over 100,000 times every day. Either out of fear or excitement, no doubt you've felt your heart "skip a beat," or race momentarily. But, for the most part, your heart beats evenly—in a steady rhythm—thanks to the heart's sophisticated electrical system. Sometimes, though, the electrical system goes awry, causing the heart to beat unevenly, or out of rhythm. This is called an arrhythmia. While some arrhythmias are perfectly harmless, others are dangerous, and can cause the heart to stop beating altogether (called a cardiac arrest).

Omega-3s are thought to guard against these bad heart rhythms, fortifying heart muscle against unstable beats. Scientists have found several ways that these healthy fats may work in the body to provide this protection. Some of these involve the way our heart's electrical system drives the heart muscle to contract, which pushes the blood out to supply oxygen to our body. Tiny channels in the outer walls of the heart muscle cells allow substances such as calcium and sodium into and out of the cell; this is what drives the muscle cells to contract. Sometimes situations such as stress can cause some of these channels to stop working properly, meaning the heart won't contract as it is supposed to. The omega-3 fats seem to help these channels keep working properly, even when we are under stress. The good news for those of you who don't eat fish is that one of the ways omega-3s may help stabilize our heart's electrical system is aided by plant sources of omega-3s (the flaxseed, walnuts, canola oil, and so on) as well as by the omega-3s found in fish. And the great news for those of you who do enjoy fish is that just one fish meal per week has been shown to have this stabilizing ability.

Omega-3s reduce blood pressure

Omega-3s help drop blood pressure readings. Although it's not a very large effect, and omega-3s won't replace your blood pressure medication if you have significantly high readings, this effect is still valuable. When blood pressure is too high, it damages the artery walls, making them a magnet for artery-narrowing plaques. Raised blood pressure also increases your risk of stroke.

While scientists have found a few different reasons why the healthy fish fats may reduce blood pressure, one of them comes down to the eicosanoid chemicals again. By shifting the balance in our diet to more

omega-3s and less omega-6s, we shift the eicosanoid balance from con-
stricting or squeezing blood vessels to allowing them to relax. Thus,
our blood pressure is reduced.

Omega-3s bump up levels of the good cholesterol, HDL

High levels of HDL help stop artery-clogging heart disease by keeping
the LDL or "bad" cholesterol from narrowing our arteries. Research
has found that taking in more omega-3s can bring small increases in
the levels of this protective blood fat. In fact, eating fish keeps HDL-
cholesterol from dropping, as it often does when people change to a
lower-fat diet.

With all the different actions of omega-3s to protect our hearts,
some of the great benefits we reap from these healthy fats are:

- Reduced risk of sudden death from heart attack. Several large
  scientific studies showed that people who had the highest intake
  of omega-3 fats in their diets were less likely to die suddenly
  from a sudden heart attack.
- If you've had a blockage cleared from your arteries, or bypass
  surgery, getting enough omega-3 may prevent the artery from
  closing again (called restenosis).

And, if you've been unfortunate enough to have had a heart attack,
it's not too late to help yourself with omega-3s, as they:

- Protect against a second heart attack. Having enough omega-3s
  can reduce your risk of suffering a second, fatal heart attack.

How Much Omega-3 Do We Need?

Whether or not you have been diagnosed with heart disease will affect
how much omega-3 fat you should try to eat each day. It may also be
advisable to aim for a higher amount if you have high triglyceride levels—you should discuss this with your physician.

How much omega-3s to protect against heart disease?

As we read in the last chapter, the American Heart Association recommends having a minimum of two fish meals each week (mostly choosing types of fish that are higher in omega-3s) for people who have not been diagnosed with heart disease. In addition, they recommend choosing oils and margarines that are higher in omega-3s, such as those made from canola or soybean oil.

If you don't eat fish, you will need to concentrate a bit harder on your diet and eat at least 3 to 4 grams per day of omega-3s from plant sources; this should provide your body with approximately the same amount of EPA and DHA (the fish-type omega-3s) as two oily fish meals a week. (Do remember, however, that scientists are not completely sure exactly how much of the plant omega-3s get converted to the fish-type omega-3s in our bodies.) You can find out how to do this in Chapter 4, and there's a two-week menu and many delicious recipes especially for you in Chapter 8.

How much omega-3 if I already have heart disease?

Experts agree that you require more omega-3s to combat already-existing heart disease than you need simply to protect against developing it. This simply requires a lot more attention to your diet if you eat fish, but unfortunately this makes it virtually impossible to eat enough omega-3s only from plant sources.

If you have heart disease, the American Heart Association recommends an intake of the fish-type omega-3s of about 1 gram per day, which is equivalent to eating oily fish about once daily. Remember that it doesn't always have to be a main meal. Tuna-fish sandwiches for lunch and sardines on toast for breakfast also count as fish meals, so fish once a day is easier than you'd think. It does get a lot more difficult if you don't eat fish, as you'd probably need to take in at least 10 to 15 grams of omega-3s from plants each day for your body to produce 1 gram of EPA and DHA. (Again, remember that no one is exactly sure how much omega-3 our body will convert from the plant type to the fish type). Try some of the high-omega-3 recipes in the last chapter, and check through the food sources of omega-3s in Chapter 4 for ideas.

Whether fish is on your menu or not, you might find it difficult to take in enough omega-3s to combat heart disease. If you are having trouble, you may wish to discuss fish oil supplements with your doctor. You can read more about these supplements in Chapter 4.

How much omega-3 if I have high triglycerides?

Scientists have found that the amount of omega-3s required to reduce high triglyceride levels are larger than the amounts needed to battle heart disease without high triglyceride levels. The amount recommended by the American Heart Association is 2 to 4 grams of EPA and DHA each day, or two to four times the amounts for people with heart disease. As you can imagine, it is not really possible to eat this amount from a regular diet.

If you have high triglyceride levels, ask your doctor whether fish-oil supplements could be useful for you. Do not take them without discussing it with your doctor first as, at this high level of intake, they may not be suitable for some people or they may interact with other medications you are taking.

Omega-3s: Heart-healthy for You and Me

From Eskimos in Greenland to the American heartland, we have all realized the benefits of omega-3s to keep our hearts ticking. I know they have helped me to control my cholesterol levels and blood pressure, thus reducing my risk of heart disease. I hope you can enjoy more fish and other omega-3 foods in your diet and reap the same benefits.

Chapter 3

Omega-3s and the Prevention of Other Conditions Affecting the Body and Mind

We know that omega-3 fats can protect us against developing heart disease, and even reduce our risk of a second heart attack if we've been unfortunate enough to have a first one. And we've learnt that omega-3s are essential to our general well-being. It's also well known that fish is brain food; in this chapter you'll see how true this old saying is. But did you know the precious and essential fats from fish may bring many, many more health advantages, from reducing the pain of rheumatoid arthritis, to preventing the confusion of dementia, to reducing the weight loss that often occurs when people have cancer? How can such a simple thing as a type of fat be associated with such a huge variety of benefits? Read on, and in this chapter you'll discover that there are many reasons other than heart disease to increase your intake of omega-3s.

Because there are quite a lot of medical conditions I want to tell you about, I've divided them into three groups (leaving out the heart disease, also stroke and high blood pressure, as they were discussed in the previous chapter):

- Inflammatory disorders, including arthritis, ulcerative colitis, Crohn's disease, and psoriasis
- Moods and mental function, including the surprising links between fish and omega-3 intake and depression, dementia, and cognitive function in older adults
- Other disorders, which include cancer, diabetes, and even menstrual pain

First, however, I want to take a step back and look at how important the omega-3s are to our bodies before we even leave the womb.

Omega-3s at the Beginning of Life

The popular saying that a woman is eating for two during pregnancy couldn't be more true! And if mom breastfeeds, she is also eating for two after the birth. The mother's diet has a great influence on the general health of her baby, since he or she is dependent on mom for the nutrients and essential fatty acids needed to grow optimally. Fatty acids, especially of the omega-3 type, are critically important throughout pregnancy and when breastfeeding for the health of both the baby and the mother.

Omega-3s before birth

For baby before birth, omega-3s play important roles in:

- Normal development of his or her brain and nervous system: remember, the brain is 60% fat, so when baby is building a healthier brain, it demands omega-3s (and the other, more plentiful, essential fat, omega-6)
- How she or he will see later in life, as they are an essential part of developing eye tissue
- Growing to an optimal birth weight, a need that starts very early in pregnancy. Omega-3s help "build" the placenta, through which all the nutrients and oxygen pass from mother to baby. Thus, a healthy placenta is crucial for the baby's growth and development.

Remember how we finally determined that Eskimos had less heart disease because they ate more omega-3-rich fish? Well, we have learned from moms-to-be in Greece that eating fish lowers the chance that the baby will develop cerebral palsy; this further supports just how important omega-3s are in the baby's brain and nerve development.

And, we learned from expectant moms in the Faroe Islands (north of the United Kingdom) that eating just one more fish meal a week may help expectant moms to grow healthier weight babies—which translates into better health after birth. Researchers studied the fish-eating habits of 1,022 expectant moms and then compared that to the sizes of their babies. The more fish they ate—up to three times per week—the larger and longer the babies were likely to be. Babies of moms who enjoyed the most fish were, on average, nearly a half pound heavier and a centimeter longer than other babies. Researchers speculate that omega-3s encourage better blood flow from the mother to the placenta—and that means the baby gets more nutrients. Another explanation: omega-3s might prevent early labor and delivery by decreasing the type of prostaglandin (one of those eicosanoid chemicals we looked at in Chapter 1) that, among other jobs, initiates the uterine contractions that announce labor.

Omega-3s after the birth

Remember that the omega-3s still play a key role for babies after birth (and, indeed, through the rest of their life). Although baby formulas have long been fortified with vitamins and minerals, they often lack the omega-3s that are building blocks for the baby's brain and retinal tissue, which is still growing and fine-tuning its architecture. Mother's breast milk has up to 30 times more DHA (one of the fish omega-3s) than formula, however how much it contains depends very much on how much is in mom's diet.

Being sure to provide the right kind of nutrients and essential fatty acids is important because of the speed at which the infant's brain develops: An average newborn's brain weighs 700 grams, and by the end of the first year it has increased to 1,000 grams! The DHA is so important to a child's development that a deficiency could impede the development of the child's nervous and immune system, which might first be noticed as unexplained emotional and/or learning and attention deficit/hyperactivity disorders. Omega-3s affect the parts of the brain responsible for learning ability, anxiety/depression, and auditory and visual perception. Studies have found that breast-fed children tend to have a higher IQ and better visual function than those fed only with formula. Researchers have suggested that a lower intake of DHA of formula-fed babies may be partly responsible.

Omega-3s also benefit infants and children in other ways: it is possible that a lack of omega-3 fatty acids may cause or contribute to allergies and infections that often affect young children:

- Epstein Barr—a viral infection
- Sinus allergies
- Chronic ear, nose, and throat infections

Which omega-3s benefit babies

I have mentioned DHA, one of the omega-3s found in fish, several times already in this chapter. The reason is that DHA is the omega-3 thought to be particularly crucial to healthy brain development in babies. Therefore, researchers believe, eating fish is especially important during pregnancy and when breastfeeding (as the more DHA in mom's diet, the more will reach her baby through her breastmilk). Yes, we can get omega-3s through plants such as flax and walnuts, but you'll remember from Chapter 1 that the body only converts a small amount of the plant omega-3s to the EPA and DHA found in fish. Of the omega-3 converted, more is made into EPA than is made into the DHA needed by babies. Thus, if you do eat fish, be sure to enjoy plenty of it during pregnancy and when breastfeeding (and afterwards to rebuild your own omega-3 levels). If you don't eat fish, you will need to be very diligent with your diet to take in an optimal amount of the plant-based omega-3 fat. You could also consider including some "omega-3 eggs" in your diet, as they are a non-fish source of DHA. You can find out more about them in Chapter 6.

You may have read in the media about health concerns regarding the amount of mercury and some other chemicals in fish. There are certain types of fish that should be avoided by pregnant and breastfeeding women for this reason, including swordfish and tilefish. The

FDA also has an overall recommended limit to the amount of fish you should consume weekly (which does allow between two and four servings each week, more than many of us would eat anyway). If you fall into these categories, or you are planning to become pregnant, read the information on this subject in Chapter 5 to help you plan your fish intake.

In the omega-3 aspect of babies' health, as in many others, the experts are unanimous in their recommendation that breast is best. However, some women are not able to breastfeed their babies for a variety of reasons. If you do need to use baby formula, be sure to choose one of the newer varieties that include the essential omega-3 fats, especially DHA. You'll be pleased to hear that this is actually recommended by none less than the World Health Organisation.

Omega-3s and the Power to Calm Inflammation

We learned in Chapter 1 that omega-3s exert a lot of their benefits through their effect on the eicosanoid chemicals. We'll be learning more about these benefits in this section, so I'll remind you that these chemicals can be produced from either the omega-3 fats we take in or from the omega-6s. Those produced from the omega-6s tend to be more "aggressive" and promote, for example, inflammation, blood clotting, and blood vessel constriction. Conversely, the eicosanoids produced from the omega-3s tend to reduce inflammation and blood clotting, and allow blood vessels to relax. Obviously, since this section is about omega-3s power to calm inflammation, we'll be talking about the anti-inflammatory eicosanoid effects here.

There is another group of inflammatory chemicals at work in the body, and I'm afraid I have a few more long names to introduce. The cytokines, like the eicosanoids, are a group of hormone-like substances; the ones we're most interested in are interleukin and tumor necrosis factor (TNF). Again, like the eicosanoids, their action can be modified by the omega-3 fats in our diet. There are several types of interleukin, with slightly different actions, but, to save confusion, when I refer to interleukins I'll just be referring to those with inflammatory activity.

Although we are only talking about one effect, reducing inflammation, it may lead to relief from, or reduction of, a wide range of troubling medical conditions, from skin conditions such as psoriasis to breathing problems like asthma. Some of these diseases, including proriasis, rheumatoid arthritis, and the inflammatory bowel diseases are known as autoimmune conditions—you can read more about this later in the chapter.

Rheumatoid arthritis: how do omega-3s help?

One of the best-known effects of omega-3s is in reducing the crippling pain that characterizes rheumatoid arthritis. This is thought to be due to omega-3s effects on the inflammatory substances in the body, including the eicosanoid leukotriene, which we read about in Chapter 1, and some of the cytokines. Again, this effect is more closely related to eating fish rather than plant omega-3s, as those from fish are the omega-3s that modulate eicosanoid actions. In addition, the fish omega-3s suppress the body's production of the inflammatory cytokines, TNF and interleukin.

Researchers have looked at a number of groups of people, and related their fish intake to rheumatoid arthritis. For example, studies have shown that:

- There is a lower incidence of rheumatoid arthritis in populations that enjoy larger amounts of fish in their diet, such as the Japanese and Eskimos.
- Within a group of people, those who eat more fish have a lower likelihood of developing rheumatoid arthritis—this was found by researchers looking at the diet of people a bit closer to home, a group of women in Seattle, Washington.

Not only does eating fish reduce your chance of getting rheumatoid arthritis, it can also help relieve your symptoms if you already have this problem. Arthritis experts have found that, in just three months, people who took in the most omega-3s started to feel less pain. By the end of a year, most had a stronger grip and nearly half were able to decrease their intake of non-steroidal anti-inflammatory drugs (medications often used to treat arthritis).

Do please note that some studies showing an improvement in rheumatoid arthritis with increased amounts of omega-3s have used fish-oil supplements containing up to 3 grams of EPA and DHA daily. If you are considering trying fish-oil supplements, read the information about them in the next chapter and speak with your physician first.

Omega-3s to breathe easier: asthma, lung disease and smokers, and cystic fibrosis

Children who eat fish more than once a week have just one-third the risk of asthma of children who do not eat fish regularly. Why would this be? Again, as you learned in Chapter 2, omega-3s from fish change the type of eicosanoid chemicals the body produces. The leukotrienes are the eicosanoids particularly influential in the overly-active throat inflammation found in asthma. In addition, in asthma, the airway is called hyper-responsive, meaning that it tends to constrict too much, restricting the space the breath can pass through. The cytokine TNF plays a major role in this. The omega-3 fats act in both these areas: they decrease the production of TNF, thus making the airways less likely to constrict, and also shift leukotriene production to the more calming type that does not promote throat inflammation. This eases the wheezing and shortness of breath that asthma sufferers know all too well.

Another point about fish and lung function: While one could never say that it is good for people to smoke, we do know that fish may protect smokers from getting chronic lung problems such as emphysema. As with asthma, the omega-3 action on leukotrienes, interleukins, and TNF protects the lungs against the inflammation that is a factor in these lung diseases. While stopping smoking is always the best idea, this is good news for smokers, and an extra incentive to make omega-3s an important part of your diet.

People with cystic fibrosis may also benefit from increased omega-3s. A study has shown that supplementation of this essential fat could improve breathing and reduce the production of the thick mucus that chokes the airways of people who suffer from this debilitating condition. Again, it's important to remember that anyone taking fish-oil supplements should discuss it with their physician first.

Smoother, less itchy skin: omega-3s help psoriasis

The Eskimos of Greenland, who eat lots of fish high in omega-3 fatty acids, rarely have psoriasis. While not painful, psoriasis can be devastatingly disfiguring—so disfiguring that sufferers might be very happy to eat one fish meal a day. That's how much it takes—the equivalent of one 3-ounce salmon, sardine or mackerel meal daily, in conjunction with a psoriasis medication called etretinate—to experience good improvement. Incidentally, psoriasis patients are benefited in another way: etretinate tends to raise blood triglyceride levels, and the fish fat brings them down.

I am not a great fan of fish-oil capsules unless they're really necessary—if possible, always go for the real fillet (or flaxseeds, walnuts, greens or soy foods) to get your omega-3s. According to the National Psoriasis Foundation, most studies using fish-oil capsules to help psoriasis found no benefit. However, in one British study, psoriasis patients ate 5 ½ ounces of fatty fish daily—and they experienced improvement of psoriasis symptoms.

IBD and omega-3s: can they help Crohn's disease and ulcerative colitis?

IBD stands for inflammatory bowel disease; in practice this includes Crohn's disease and ulcerative colitis, two chronic conditions that cause severe inflammation and ulceration of parts of the digestive tract. The inflammation can be so severe that sometimes a portion of the bowel may have to be surgically removed. Because they are caused by inflammation, and because omega-3s have proved helpful in other inflammatory conditions, it stands to reason that they may be helpful in these illnesses, too.

A study of patients with Crohn's disease found that fish-oil supplements actually reduced the amount of relapses of this condition. As with the other diseases above, it's thought that the omega-3s altered the type of eicosanoids produced to the less inflammatory versions, and suppressed the production of TNF.

Omega-3s have also been shown to benefit people with ulcerative colitis; a study actually demonstrated that there was a change from the more to the less aggressive form of the inflammatory eicosanoid leukotriene (I hope all these long names are becoming more familiar to you now). More importantly for people with ulcerative colitis, they had less problems from the disease. They were able to gain some weight (as you'd imagine, weight loss is a regular feature of the condition) and they spent less time in the bathroom.

Do note that the people in the study took relatively large amounts of fish oil, 2.7 grams per day in the Crohn's disease study and about twice as much in the ulcerative colitis research, over a long term period. Most people are unlikely to manage to eat this amount of fish in a day, as 2.7 grams of fish oil is the equivalent of several fish meals, so supplements would generally be required to achieve this intake. Of course you remember that you should talk with your physician before taking fish-oil supplements.

Menstrual pain and headaches

The discomfort associated with menstruation may not seem like a major medical condition compared to those we've been discussing, but it provides yet another example of the many ways omega-3s can improve our lives. It is a different eicosanoid causing the inflammation this time: prostaglandin. The omega-3 seems to come to the rescue in the same way we've heard before though—by changing the type of prostaglandin produced, from the more inflammatory one that produces, for example, muscle spasm, to the milder one that allows our muscles to relax.

Omega-3s Use in Hospitals

As a dietitian, I am not just concerned with preventing illness in people who are well. My role extends to the nutritional care of people who are very ill. Omega-3s have a part to play here as well.

Research has shown, for example, that the fish-based omega-3s can help to calm the body processes that lead people with pancreatic cancer, a very aggressive cancer, to lose weight so quickly. Dietitians and other health professionals are trying to use this knowledge to help people with cancer feel stronger and even live longer.

The omega-3s are also being used to help people having major surgery in hospitals. Studies have found that patients who took nutritional supplements that contained omega-3s and a few other special nutrients had less infections and wound-healing complications after major operations. Researchers think this may be due to a combination of omega-3s immune-boosting and anti-inflammatory properties.

Omega-3s: Their Role in Mood and Mental Function

We've learned a lot about the different and beneficial effects of the omega-3s on our body; now we're going to look at their effects on our mind. Your mother probably told you fish was brain food, and she was right! You'll recall that fish-type omega-3s are particularly important for the healthy development of a baby's brain and nervous system. Well they seem to go on being a major factor in healthy brain function, from childhood through to old age.

Compelling new evidence suggests that the omega-3s may explain why the Eskimos of Greenland were thought to be "even keeled," or relatively untroubled. Indeed, omega-3s are thought to have several benefits on the brain. Today, we understand that this makes sense, given that 60% of the brain is fat—a significant portion of which is omega-3s. A growing list of studies supports the hypothesis of a link between the intake of omega-3s and psychiatric diseases. Unlike many antidepressant medications such as Prozac, which can cause nausea, sexual dysfunction, and other troubling side effects, omega-3s from food probably do not have negative side-effects.

Some of the benefits on mental health of omega-3s include:

- Lowering the risk of major depression: Research shows that people who have depression and suicidal tendencies eat fewer omega-3 rich foods.
- Help in the management of bipolar disorder
- Decreasing aggressive and impulsive behaviours in people with these tendencies
- Lower levels of hyperactivity in schoolchildren
- Reducing the risk of dementia, one form of which is Alzheimer's disease: Research has shown that people who have Alzheimer's often have lower levels of one of the fish-type omega-3s (DHA) in their blood than people who do not have this disease of aging.

How omega-3s might help in mental health

Omega-3s are thought to help mental health by making it easier for brain cells to pass mood-related signals—messages—to each other. Brain cells are called neurons, and the process of passing messages is called transmission. Omega-3s help neurons transmit messages more efficiently. For example, researchers think that omega-3s may correct the chaotic and confusing manner in which brain cells transfer messages to one another in people who have bipolar disorder, which evens out moods.

Omega-3s and children's behavior

Could eating fish make your children behave and learn better in school? Research leads us to think that this simple dietary change could have such a profound effect. Researchers in the US looked at the amount of omega-3 fat versus the amount of omega-6 fat in the blood of schoolchildren. They found that those with lower levels of omega-3 fat were more likely to have either behavioral or learning problems; the behavioral problems included hyperactivity, disturbed sleep and, what every parent dreads, more temper tantrums. Does this mean eating more fish will help our kids to learn and behave better? We can't be sure without more research. But given the myriad of other health benefits from eating omega-3-rich fish and plant foods, it seems reasonable to consider offering fish to our children more frequently.

If your kids aren't keen on the idea of a fillet of fish for dinner, they might prefer sardines on toast for breakfast, a tuna or salmon sandwich for lunch, or tuna casserole for dinner. Check the guidelines on safe intakes of fish for children in Chapter 5.

Omega-3s to lift your spirits: fighting depression

An Australian study of people who were clinically depressed found that those with more severe depression tended to have more omega-6-type fat in their blood and less omega-3-type fat. These researchers then went on to compare entire populations. They found that people from countries that eat lower amounts of fish, such as West Germany, have a higher chance of being depressed than people from countries such as Japan, where fish intake is much higher. Just a coincidence? Scientists don't think so. But they also think they know why this might happen, why a lower intake of omega-3s might be linked to depression. Again, it's related to the fish-type omega-3 fat's modulation of the eicosanoids and cytokines. It's thought that these chemicals are involved in an immune response that, in turn, alters the body's hormones to make us more prone to depression.

One type of depression that has received a great deal of exposure is postpartum depression. Not surprisingly, an inadequate intake of omega-3s late in pregnancy, when your growing baby is demanding so much from you, may be a factor in postnatal depression after the birth. So, if you are pregnant, be sure to have enough fish or plant omega-3s to keep you and your baby not only healthy but also happy.

Omega-3s and older adults: improving mental function and reducing dementia

Alzheimer's disease and other dementias are greatly feared diseases of aging, and omega-3s are thought to protect the brain from developing dementia by:

- Keeping the brain's blood vessels squeaky clean by preventing "junk" from clogging the inside of them and preventing dangerous blood clots from forming. In turn, this means the brain gets more oxygen-rich blood flowing to it, which keeps it healthier.
- Stopping the body's production of inflammatory substances: If you are in-the-know about the topic of Alzheimer's disease, you may have read or heard that when this disease affects the brain, it causes an inflammatory reaction. The anti-inflammatory omega-3 action you've heard about so many times may suppress this.
- Scientists theorise that omega-3s may also play a role in the regeneration of damaged nerve cells.

That's the theory about how omega-3 fats may protect against dementia; have they been shown to do so in practice? Yes; research does seem to back up these theories. A study reported in the prestigious British Medical Journal looked at 1,674 people aged 68 or over. Those who ate fish at least once a week had a significantly lower risk of developing dementia over the seven years of the study. In another study by researchers at the National Institutes of Health, of more than 1,000 people (average age 75), those with higher blood levels of the fish-type omega-3 DHA were more than 40% less likely to develop dementia (including Alzheimer's) over the next nine years than people with low DHA levels.

In addition to protecting our mental function against dementia, omega-3s may also prevent a loss of mental function as we age. A study of older adults in the Netherlands showed that those who took in more omega-3 fats experienced less mental decline than those who consumed more omega-6 fats.

Omega-3s: Other Health Benefits

We've talked about so many areas already where omega-3s may either make us healthier or help our body to better manage challenging health problems. But there are yet more areas in which research has revealed the fabulous benefits of omega-3s.

Resisting cancer with omega-3s

Nutrition experts have long-advised us to reduce intake of all fat, especially animal fat, to lessen the risk of cancers, especially breast and colorectal cancer. "There's now excellent evidence that eating fish provides protection against colorectal cancers," says Bandaru S. Reddy, Ph.D., chief of the division of nutritional carcinogenesis at the American Health Foundation in Valhalla, New York. Studying 24 European populations, British researchers found that the oil in fish somehow protects against the detrimental effects of animal fat that lead to cancer. They estimated that decreasing animal fat by 15% would decrease the chances of dying from colorectal cancer by 6%. More remarkably, they also estimated that adding 3 fish meals weekly—in addition to decreasing animal fat by 15%—would slash the male death rate from colorectal cancer by nearly one-third. Researchers in Italy studied over 18,000 people, looking at factors that influenced the development of cancer. Again the results were in favor of eating more fish, as only small amounts seemed to reduce cancer risk, especially for cancers of the digestive tract, which of course includes the all-too-common colorectal cancer. The same result came from researchers at Harvard studying nearly 90,000 nurses—more fish was related to less colon cancer. In addition, scientists believe that more omega-3s may help to guard against breast cancer and prostate cancers, though scientific studies show mixed results with both these types of cancer.

How might fish oil fight cancer? We're back to the prostaglandin connection, says Dr. Reddy. The omega-3s change the type of prostaglandin (you'll remember that this is one of the eicosanoids) made by the body, again leading the body to produce less of the aggressive types and more of a less aggressive, more calming kind. This benefits the body when it comes to fighting cancer, because prostaglandins are called tumor promoters—they can be substances that encourage cancer tumors to grow.

Omega-3s: fighting back when our immune system fights too hard

You may wonder when an immune system could fight too hard—surely we need it to fight as hard as possible to protect our body from invading bacteria and viruses. The problem lies when it is no longer just protecting the body but also attacking it. In other words, some health conditions can put us under "friendly-fire;" they are called "auto-immune" conditions. Scientists think that omega-3s may help to "turn down" this immune over-reaction, possibly leading to easing of auto-immune diseases.

One such condition is lupus, more correctly known as lupus erythematosus, or LE. It's a condition I know very well, as I do battle with it every day of my life. Thus, I also know that omega-3s have helped me to fight it. Lupus can range from a more manageable skin condition, to a disorder in which virtually any part of the body can come under attack. One of the characteristics of lupus is the presence of one of the eicosanoids, the proinflammatory form of leukotriene, and also of the inflammatory cytokine interleukin. Since we know that omega-3s reduce the production of the cytokine interleukin and push production of leukotriene toward the less inflammatory form, it doesn't seem surprising that people who've taken fish oils in scientific studies have frequently seen an improvement in their condition. I know I have.

Note that rheumatoid arthritis, the inflammatory bowel diseases, and psoriasis are also sparked off by an "auto-immune" element as well as having their inflammatory side. Other health conditions that share some of these characteristics and may also be helped by omega-3s include multiple sclerosis and migraine headaches.

Omega-3s: benefits in diabetes

Omega-3s serve up a fabulous array of benefits for people with diabetes. In fact, research in Finland and the Netherlands shows they may actually reduce the risk of developing type 2 diabetes, the more common type that tends to strike in middle to older age. However, if you do have diabetes, here are the benefits that tasty tuna and scrumptious salmon could bring you:

- Omega-3 fats are thought to help insulin work better. Insulin helps the body to control blood sugar levels by taking the sugar or glucose out of the blood and into the body's cells through the cell wall. Diabetes occurs when either the body isn't producing enough insulin, or it isn't working as well as it should, a condition called "insulin resistance." Scientists think that omega-3s may combat this insulin resistance, helping insulin to work more efficiently in controlling blood sugar levels. They know that omega-3 fats are a part of cell walls or membranes, and that having more omega-3s makes the membrane more "fluid." This may make the insulin "receptors" in the cell wall more receptive to the insulin, helping the insulin to work better, and thus helping people with diabetes to have better control of their blood sugar levels.
- The essential omega-3s reduce the risk of heart disease, which is more likely in people with diabetes.

- Fish oils help lower triglyceride levels, which are often raised in people with diabetes and lead to further increases in the risk of heart disease. (As discussed in the last chapter, this benefit generally requires a higher amount of omega-3 fat than we can easily take in from our diet, so a supplement may be required. See the note of caution at the end of this list).
- The level of HDL (the "good" cholesterol) tends to rise with a higher intake of omega-3s. This valuable type of cholesterol, which is low in some people with diabetes, protects our arteries against the build up of "sludge" that is seen in heart disease.
- Omega-3 fats can reduce blood pressure. Again, this is often high in people with diabetes and is another risk factor for heart disease.
- Fish oils may prevent or delay the kidney failure that can occur in people with diabetes by keeping blood vessels stronger and less "leaky."

I will add one note of caution: It is best to get your omega-3s from natural sources rather than supplements if possible, and this is particularly true if you have diabetes. That's because some research has shown that taking in large amounts of fish oil, amounts that may be consumed if you are taking supplements, can cause poorer control of blood sugar levels. In other words, your blood sugars could rise higher. While this certainly hasn't been found in all studies or in all people, the overall advice remains the same: always see your doctor before taking a fish-oil supplement.

Osteoporosis: omega-3s keeping bones strong

In yet another omega-3 breakthrough, scientists are looking at whether omega-3 fats can help to slow the rapid bone loss that occurs when a woman goes through menopause. Incredibly, unless she takes hormone replacement therapy, it's not uncommon for a women to lose 15% of her bone mass in the five years following menopause. This frequently translates to osteoporosis in later life; more than 50% of women over 80 years old have suffered compression fractures of their spine.

When I tell you that several of the inflammatory cytokines are implicated in causing this rapid bone loss, and that prostaglandins influence how quickly our bone is built up or broken down, you'll be able to see why scientists think omega-3s may be useful in preventing osteoporosis. Researchers have found the positive results of omega-3s in laboratory tests, in studies with animals, and in most of the studies they've carried out to look at women's bones and the amount of omega-3 fat in their diets. These were small studies, and they were carried out over a short period of time, so there is certainly more research needed. However, scientists are cautiously optimistic that a diet including plenty of omega-3 fat, and not too much omega-6 fat, could help to keep our bones stronger into old age.

Omega-3s in kidney failure and kidney transplant

We don't spend a lot of time thinking about our kidneys, though they are always working for us, filtering waste products out of our blood, making sure we have the right amount of water in our body, and helping regulate our blood pressure. We usually only notice them when something goes wrong and, as you can imagine given the kidney's essential functions, this is very serious indeed. One of the most common yet serious disorders involving the kidneys is a condition called IgA nephropathy, which causes progressively poorer kidney function, and usually results in kidney failure within 10 to 20 years. When kidney failure occurs, either dialysis or a kidney transplant is necessary to prevent death.

There are no cures for IgA nephropathy, however omega-3 fats have shown great promise in slowing the disease's progression. In one study of 106 patients with this disorder, 55 were given fish-oil supplements. When researchers looked at the groups four years later, a massive 40% of the group not taking the supplements had either died or reached kidney failure. Contrast this with the people taking the supplements, of whom only 10% had died or reached kidney failure. It seems amazing that something so simple as fish oil could have such a profound effect on people's lives.

Omega-3s can also offer help to another group of people with kidney problems: those undergoing a kidney transplant. Researchers have found a variety of benefits if people take fish-oil supplements following their transplant, including better blood flow through the new kidney, better kidney function, and less cases of rejection of the transplanted kidney. Again, another omega-3 benefit that can literally save lives.

But Wait . . . There'll Be More

Expect to read much, much more about the benefits of omega-3s and the health advantages of eating fish regularly. Scientists are doing more research in a huge range of areas, including those we've talked about and other areas such as:

- multiple sclerosis
- schizophrenia
- chronic fatigue syndrome
- premenstrual syndrome
- eczema
- macular degeneration (the most common cause of blindness in the elderly) and
- Raynaud's disease (a circulatory problem causing cold hands and feet)

They are looking for more information about which medical conditions omega-3s can aid or help to prevent, and trying to find out exactly how this crucial nutrient works with the body to bring those benefits.

I personally know that including omega-3-rich fish or plant foods as a frequent part of your diet does more than reduce your risk of heart disease. As I told you in the Introduction, I personally have benefited in ways ranging from reducing the inflammation that provokes my asthma and psoriasis to calming my immune system to help keep my lupus in check. While I do hope none of you are combating the range of health problems that I am every day, I'm sure everyone has problems they want to keep in check, or at the least, prevent developing in the first place. So read on to find out exactly what are the best and richest sources of omega-3s, both in and out of the sea, and how to make them a regular and delicious feature on your dinner table.

Chapter 4

Omega-3 Sources: Thoughts on Supplements and Food Charts

Whether you like fish or not, you can get plenty of omega-3s! Chapters 5 and 6 will provide a wealth of information on buying, storing, and, most importantly, cooking both fish and the plant sources of omega-3s. In this chapter, you'll find a lot more detail on exactly how much of this essential fat is in these sources. I list other important nutrients in the charts, and I'll explain these before we get to the charts. Also, we'll look at the issue of taking fish-oil supplements.

Before we look at omega-3 sources, let's recap how much the American Heart Association recommends we have each day of this essential fat:

- If you do not have heart disease, eat at least two fish-based meals each week, usually focusing on the oily, higher omega-3 fish. This will provide approximately 2 grams or more of the fish-type omega-3s each week. Also, include high omega-3 plant sources in your diet where possible, for example by choosing cooking oils and margarines based on canola oil. Although we can't be sure exactly how much of the plant-type omega-3, alpha linolenic acid, gets converted by our body to the more valuable EPA and DHA, the fish-type omega-3s, we know it isn't much. Thus, I suggest you aim to take in at least 3 to 4 grams of plant omega-3s every day if you don't include fish in your diet.
- If you have been diagnosed with heart disease, the recommendation is to consume approximately 1 gram of EPA/DHA every day from fish. If you don't eat fish, you probably need to take in at least 10 to 15 grams of omega-3s from plants each day. You may find that this isn't practical for you and that you can't reach

these levels from the foods you eat, particularly if you don't eat fish. Please take what omega-3s you can from your diet, but you may wish to consider a supplement.

- If you have high triglyceride levels, 2 to 4 grams of EPA/DHA (which would need to be provided as a supplement) have been shown to help in lowering them.

Also, as you read in the previous chapter, you may with to take higher amounts of omega-3s if you have conditions such as rheumatoid arthritis. I'd like to emphasize again that anyone thinking about taking supplements should discuss this with their physician first.

The Skinny on Supplements

If possible, I'd really prefer you to get your omega-3s from foods rather than supplements. There are two major reasons. Firstly, sometimes people who take supplements feel they can get away with eating a less healthy diet, and this is just not the case. Eating unhealthily will negate the beneficial effects of the fish oils. Secondly, the fish and plant foods high in omega-3s contribute so many other valuable nutrients to our diet, and I don't want anyone to miss out on them. That said, sometimes it can just be too difficult to eat enough omega-3s, especially if you don't eat fish. And if you are unlucky enough to already have heart disease or high triglyceride levels, you may find you need to take supplements even if you do eat fish. Alternatively, you may be able to compromise and eat a higher omega-3 diet on some days of the week and take fish-oil supplements on the other days. Just always remember the golden rule: don't take fish-oil supplements unless you have discussed them with your physician.

There are two types of fish oil-type supplements on the market: those made from fish livers, such as cod liver oil, and those containing the oil from fish bodies. To be clear, I'm going to call the latter "fish oils," and the first "fish liver oils." Just as the liver is very different to the rest of a fish body, so the oils are quite different. The fish liver oil contains large amounts of vitamins A and D, but not so much of the omega-3s EPA and DHA. In contrast, the fish oil contains much more EPA and DHA, and much less of the vitamins. While you know you need the omega-3s, do you also need these extra vitamins? The answer is generally no. In fact, the amount of vitamin A in some fish liver oils is great enough that you may risk having a dangerously high intake if you take a lot of fish liver oil. Thus, I want you to look for the fish oils, rather than the fish liver oils. However, please do look for fish-oil preparations that contain vitamin E, as it has "antioxidant" qualities and helps prevent the omega-3 fats from going "off" or "oxidizing"—you can read more about this process in Chapter 6.

A typical amount of omega-3s found in fish-oil capsules is about 180 mg of EPA and 120 mg of DHA. Together this makes 400 mg of omega-3s, or between one-third and one-half of the 1 gram (1,000 mg) recommended for people with heart disease, for example. Therefore you'd need to take three capsules of this preparation per day to meet this recommendation. Always check the label to see how much omega-3 is in the individual preparations to see how many capsules you would need.

Safety Issues and Other Concerns

With the exception of eating fish at Eskimo levels, the evidence is clear that eating fish is very safe and healthy as well as delicious and nutritious. However, there are a few safety issues that I want you to be aware of. Mostly these only become an issue if you are thinking of taking a fish-oil supplement, and only then if you are taking quite large amounts, for example if you have high triglyceride levels. The only thing to be aware of with the amounts of fish we regularly include in out diet is the increased level of mercury and some other chemicals in certain types of fish. This is particularly important information for pregnant and nursing moms and young children. Read the *Fish Facts* sidebar in Chapter 5 for more information on this.

There are more safety concerns regarding omega-3s when people take fish-oil supplements. When taken at the level equivalent to a normal fish intake, for example the 1 gram per day recommended if you have heart disease, no adverse effects should arise. However, when taken at significantly higher levels, for example the 2 to 4 grams suggested to lower triglyceride levels, it is a bit more like taking a drug. Thus, as with many drugs, there are possible side effects. Researchers have found that these can include increased bleeding (remember that omega-3s reduce our blood's tendency to clot), increases in LDL-cholesterol (the "bad" one), and reduced control of blood glucose levels in people with diabetes. The increase in bleeding has the potential to be more serious in people who take anti-clotting medications such as aspirin or warfarin. This is why I can't recommend strongly enough that you consult your physician before taking this, or any other, supplement. I don't want to cause alarm however—the FDA have given fish oils at up to 3 grams per day their "Generally Recognized As Safe" rating, after looking closely at each of the side effects I mentioned above.

If you need to take fish-oil capsules, you may have a few concerns of your own. The first is related to the taste of the tablets or, more specifically, their aftertaste. If you find the tablets are "repeating" on you, try to take them with or just following a meal. You may also be able to find some fish-oil supplements that are labeled as "enterically-coated," which means the oils will be released further down the digestive tract beyond the stomach, reducing any aftertaste. The second concern is related to the extra fat in the tablets. While just a few capsules each day might contribute, for example, 3 grams of fat to your diet, if you need to take larger amounts, which might be as much as 12 capsules or 12 grams of fat, this becomes more significant. It isn't too much extra in one day, but it is an extra 360 grams of fat each month. Over a year this could lead to quite noticeable weight gain. Thus, if you are taking larger amounts of fish-oil supplements, you will need to be extra-vigilant about eating a healthy, low-fat diet.

What Information Will I Find in These Charts?

You'll see that most of this chapter is made up of charts. They go through the richest sources of the omega-3s, both from the plant and marine world, and emphasize a number of nutrients. Here are a couple of important notes about the information in the charts:

- In each chart, you will first see a column listing an amount of omega-3. This corresponds to the *serving size,* which is in column two for the specific food *(listed in column three)*.
- Some charts list a value for additional nutrients. Those that you will see on some charts, along with the reason why, are:

  Calories: Eating just the right amount of calories each day is important to maintaining a healthy body weight. If you gain weight because you are eating foods high in omega-3s that add too many calories to your diet, then you negate a lot of the good that omega-3s do for you. So, think carefully about the amount of omega-3s you'll gain if the food is high in calories.

  Fat grams: You'll want to keep track of the total fat grams you eat to keep an overall healthy nutrition profile. Also, you'll find that although some foods seem like good sources of omega-3s, the total number of fat grams is very high—perhaps prohibitively so.

  Saturated fat: This is one type of fat within the total fat found in the serving of food noted. When eaten in excess, saturated fat is the type of fat that is most likely to cause heart disease. I list the amount of this type of fat because although total fat of a certain item might be reasonable, the saturated fat might be so high as to cause the item to be a less desirable source of omega-3s.

  Cholesterol: Cholesterol from food is also a concern when it comes to heart disease, though less so than the saturated fat discussed above. Daily cholesterol intake should be less than 300 milligrams (on average) for people who do not have heart disease (less than 200 milligrams for people who already have it), so watch out for foods that have large amounts.

Fiber: I list this for fruits, vegetables, grains, and legumes because fiber is another factor—in addition to omega-3s—that may help fight heart disease and cancer. Foods that offer a good amount of fiber along with omega-3s are truly a bonus food.

Good source of: In some cases, I note when foods are a good source of nutrients that work with or along side omega-3s to fight heart disease, cancer, and inflammatory conditions. For example:

- Potassium helps to lower blood pressure.
- Vitamin E, especially from food, might help to battle heart disease, cancer, and inflammatory conditions (such as asthma and arthritis). It also protects the valuable omega-3s against becoming rancid.
- Folate is thought to help reduce the risk of heart disease.
- Vitamin C is a powerful antioxidant that may help fight heart disease and cancer, especially when obtained from food.

The take-away message of this information is that you should strive to choose foods that have many good qualities, rather than focusing on one ingredient or substance—even a great one such as omega-3s. With that, search the charts for foods you enjoy that will help you increase your intake of omega-3s.

What About Omega-3 Eggs?

You may have seen eggs containing omega-3 fats at your supermarket. Do note that I am not talking about just any eggs; they are not naturally a good source of omega-3s. However, some chickens are fed a special diet containing elements such as linseed, fish oil or canola oil to lead them to lay eggs that contain extra omega-3 fats, and these eggs will be specially labeled as such.

(continued on next page)

"Omega-3 eggs" contain differing amounts of omega-3 fat, and you will need to check the labels or accompanying nutrition information to see just how much omega-3 (and other nutrients) the brand you are looking at contain. In general they range from about 100 mg of omega-3s per egg to about 350 mg. Of this, some will be linolenic acid (the plant-type omega-3), and some will be DHA, one of the fish-type omega-3s. One egg will probably contain about 50 to 100 mg of DHA, so one or two eggs will provide about as much fish-type omega-3 as a meal of an omega-3-rich fish.

The omega-3 eggs have a few other nutritional benefits over regular eggs:

- They are slightly lower in cholesterol than other eggs; however, like other eggs, their yolks are still a high-cholesterol food.
- They contain more vitamin E than other eggs; this has the advantage of being an antioxidant and preventing the omega-3 fat from becoming rancid and useless. Chapter 6 will explain more about how this works.
- They contain a little less saturated fat (the type that tends to raise blood cholesterol).

Omega-3 eggs are the only significant source of the valuable fish-type omega-3s for those who don't eat fish, and they may be a convenient source for anyone who eats eggs. However there are a few drawbacks. Firstly, omega-3 eggs are more expensive than regular eggs. Also, for people who are trying to control high blood cholesterol levels and limit their intake of cholesterol from food, eating these or any eggs too regularly may take you over the American-Heart-Association-recommended limit for dietary cholesterol (200 mg per day).

Fish

I've picked the best sources of omega-3 from fish by choosing those that are highest, in the most reasonable amount of fat and with minimal cholesterol. My top picks are in bold italics.

Omega-3s (grams)	Amount	Food Item	Calories	Fat (grams)	Saturated Fat (grams)	Cholesterol (milligrams)	Good source of:
1.76	3 ounces	Anchovies, Canned in oil	179	8	2	72	potassium, vitamin E
1.76	3 ounces	Anchovies, Cooked	179	8	2	72	potassium, vitamin E
0.77	3 ounces	Bass Fillet, Freshwater, Baked, Broiled	124	4	1	74	potassium
0.84	3 ounces	Bluefish Fillet, Baked, Broiled	135	5	1	65	potassium, vitamin E
1.58	3 ounces	Butterfish Fillet, Baked, Broiled	159	9	3	71	potassium
0.55	3 ounces	Calamari/Squid, Fried	149	6	2	221	potassium, vitamin E
0.68	3 ounces	Carp Fillet, Baked, Broiled	138	6	1	71	potassium, vitamin E
0.44	3 ounces	Catfish Fillet, (Channel), Breaded, Fried	195	11	3	68.89	potassium, vitamin E
5.58	3 ounces	Caviar, red or black	214	15	3	500	potassium, vitamin E
1.06	3 ounces	Cisco Fish, Smoked	151	10	1	22	potassium
0.36	3 ounces	Crab, Alaska King, Steamed, Boiled	83	1	0	45	potassium, vitamin E
0.42	3 ounces	Crab, Blue, Steamed, Boiled	87	2	0	85	potassium, vitamin E
0.69	3 ounces	Drum Fish, Freshwater Fillet, Baked, Broiled	130	5	1	70	potassium
0.63	3 ounces	Eel Fillet, Baked, Broiled	201	13	3	137	potassium, vitamin E
5.58	3 ounces	Fish Roe	214	15	4	500	potassium, vitamin E
1.05	3 ounces	Halibut Fillet, Greenland, Baked, Broiled	203	15	3	50	potassium, vitamin E
0.47	3 ounces	Halibut Fillet, Pacific, Baked, Broiled	119	3	0	35	potassium, vitamin E
1.83	3 ounces	Herring Fillet, Baked, Broiled	173	10	2	65	potassium, vitamin E
1.95	3 ounces	Herring Fillet, Smoked	185	11	2	70	potassium, vitamin E
1.18	3 ounces	Herring, Pickled	223	15	2	11	potassium, vitamin E
0.42	3 ounces	Lobster, (Spiny), Steamed, Boiled	122	2	0	77	potassium, vitamin E

Omega-3s (grams)	Amount	Food Item	Calories	Fat (grams)	Saturated Fat (grams)	Cholesterol (milligrams)	Good source of:
1.65	3 ounces	Mackerel Fillet (Pacific) Baked, Broiled	171	9	2	51	potassium
1.16	3 ounces	Mackerel Fillet (Spanish), Baked, Broiled	134	5	2	62	potassium
0.34	3 ounces	Mackerel Fillet, (King), Baked, Broiled	114	2	0	58	potassium, vitamin E
1.12	3 ounces	Mackerel Fillet, (Atlantic), Baked, Broiled	223	15	4	64	potassium, vitamin E
1.08	3 ounces	Mackerel, (Jack), Canned	133	5	2	67	potassium, vitamin E
0.7	3 ounces	Mussels, Blue, Steamed, Boiled	146	4	1	48	potassium, vitamin E
0.27	3 ounces	Octopus, Dried	139	2	0	82	potassium, vitamin E
1.22	3 ounces	Oysters, (Pacific), Steamed, Boiled	139	4	1	85	potassium, vitamin E
0.49	3 ounces	Oysters, Battered, Fried	168	11	3	69	potassium, vitamin E
0.49	3 ounces	Oysters, Eastern, Breaded, Fried	168	11	3	69	potassium, vitamin E
0.4	3 ounces	Oysters, Eastern, Canned	59	2	1	47	potassium, vitamin E
0.26	3 ounces	Oysters, Eastern, Wild, Baked, Broiled	61	2	0	42	potassium, vitamin E
1.04	3 ounces	Oysters, Eastern, Wild, Steamed, Boiled	117	4	1	89	potassium, vitamin E
0.38	3 ounces	Perch Fillet, (Atlantic), Baked, Broiled	103	2	0	46	potassium, vitamin E
0.46	3 ounces	Pollock Fillet, (Atlantic), Baked, Broiled	100	1	0	77	potassium
0.4	3 ounces	Rockfish Fillet, (Pacific), Baked, Broiled	103	2	0	37	potassium, vitamin E
1.62	3 ounces	Sablefish Fillet, Baked, Broiled	213	17	3	54	potassium
1.67	3 ounces	Sablefish, Smoked	219	17	4	54	potassium
1.57	3 ounces	Salmon Fillet, (Chinook), Baked, Broiled	196	11	3	72	potassium, vitamin E
0.72	3 ounces	Salmon Fillet, (Chum), Baked, Broiled	131	4	1	81	potassium, vitamin E
1.13	3 ounces	Salmon Fillet, Pink, Baked, Broiled	126	4	1	57	potassium, vitamin E
1.1	3 ounces	Salmon Fillet, Sockeye, Baked, Broiled	184	9	2	74	potassium, vitamin E
1.34	3 ounces	Salmon Fillet, Wild Coho, Steamed, Poached (Two key things here: Wild and the manner in which you prepare it)	156	6	1	49	potassium, vitamin E

Fish* (continued from previous page)

Omega-3s (grams)	Amount	Food Item	Calories	Fat (grams)	Saturated Fat (grams)	Cholesterol (milligrams)	Good source of:
0.95	3 ounces	Salmon Fillet, Wild Coho, Baked, Broiled	118	4	1	47	potassium, vitamin E
1.04	3 ounces	Salmon, (Chum), Canned	120	5	1	33	potassium, vitamin E
1.45	3 ounces	Salmon, Pink, Canned	118	5	1	47	potassium, vitamin E
1.06	3 ounces	Salmon, Sockeye, Canned	130	6	1	37	potassium, vitamin E
1.89	3 ounces	Salmon, Wild Atlantic, Baked, Broiled (Wild is very key here!)	155	7	1	60	potassium, vitamin E
0.38	3 ounces	Salmon/Lox, Smoked	100	4	1	20	potassium, vitamin E
1.26	3 ounces	Sardines, Canned in oil, with bone	177	10	1	121	potassium
1.59	3 ounces	Sardines, Canned in tomato sauce with bones	151	10	3	52	potassium, vitamin E
0.21	3 ounces	Scallops, Steamed, Boiled	92	3	0	27	potassium, vitamin E
0.65	3 ounces	Sea Bass Fillet, Baked, Broiled	105	2	1	45	potassium
0.41	3 ounces	Seatrout Fillet, Baked, Broiled	113	4	1	90	potassium
3.13	3 ounces	Shad Fillet, Baked, Broiled	214	15	4	82	potassium, vitamin E
0.75	3 ounces	Shark, Batter Fried	194	12	3	50	potassium, vitamin E
0.42	3 ounces	Shrimp, Batter Fried	206	10	2	151	potassium, vitamin E
0.48	3 ounces	Shrimp, Canned	102	2	0	147	potassium, vitamin E
0.55	3 ounces	Shrimp, Imitation (made from Surimi)	86	1	0	31	potassium
0.42	3 ounces	Shrimp, Large, Breaded, Fried	206	10	2	151	potassium, vitamin E
0.57	3 ounces	Shrimp, Sautéed	132	4	1	157	potassium, vitamin E
0.44	3 ounces	Sole/Flounder Fish Fillet, Baked, Broiled	100	1	0	58	potassium, vitamin E
0.71	3 ounces	Spot Fish Fillet, Baked, Broiled	134	5	2	65	potassium, vitamin E
0.84	3 ounces	Striped Bass Fillet, Baked, Broiled	105	3	1	88	potassium
0.42	3 ounces	Sturgeon, Baked, Broiled	115	4	1	65	potassium
0.36	3 ounces	Surimi Fish	84	1	0	26	potassium

Omega-3s (grams)	Amount	Food Item	Calories	Fat (grams)	Saturated Fat (grams)	Cholesterol (milligrams)	Good source of:
0.9	3 ounces	Swordfish Fillet, Baked, Broiled	132	4	1	43	potassium, vitamin E
0.77	3 ounces	Tilefish Fillet, Baked, Broiled	125	4	1	54	potassium
0.97	3 ounces	Trout Fillet, Baked, Broiled	161	7	1	63	potassium
1	3 ounces	Trout Fillet, Wild Rainbow, Baked, Broiled (Note that the "wild" part of this is key)	128	5	1	59	potassium
1.28	3 ounces	Tuna, Fresh Bluefin, Baked, Broiled	157	5	1	42	potassium, vitamin E
0.35	3 ounces	Walleye Pike Fillet, Baked, Broiled	101	1	0	94	potassium
0.4	3 ounces	Walleye Pollock Fillet, Baked, Broiled	96	1	0	82	potassium
0.58	3 ounces	White Sucker Fish Fillet, Baked, Broiled	101	3	0	45	potassium
0.79	3 ounces	White Tuna In Water, Canned	109	3	1	36	potassium, vitamin E
1.57	3 ounces	Whitefish Fillet, Baked/Broiled	146	6	1	65	potassium
0.45	3 ounces	Whiting Fillet, Baked, Broiled	97	1	0	71	potassium
0.45	3 ounces	Whiting, Baked, Broiled	97	1	0	71	potassium
0.69	3 ounces	Wolffish Fillet, (Atlantic), Baked, Broiled	105	3	0	50	potassium

*Negligible source of cholesterol

61

Nuts/Nut Butters/Nut Powders*/Nut Flours/Seeds—Common Measures*

My favorite saying when it comes to nuts and nut butters is:

"A little dab will do 'ya"

Go carefully with nuts and nut butters as they are high in fat, and measure carefully so that you avoid extra calories that can lead to weight gain and negate the benefits of omega-3s.

Note that I've included common household measures of nuts and their omega-3 level, to help you understand how ounces relate to these household measures.

Food Item	Amount	Calories	Fiber (grams)	Fat (grams)	Saturated Fat (grams)	Good source of:	Omega-3s (grams)
Almond butter	1 ounce	171	1	15	1	protein, potassium, vitamin E	0.11
Almond butter	1 ounce	180	1	17	2	protein, potassium, vitamin E	0.12
Almond butter	2 tbsp	198	1	18	2	protein, vitamin E, potassium	0.13
Almond powder	1 ounce	168	1	15	1	protein, potassium, vitamin E	0.1
Almonds, blanched	1 ounce	165	3	14	1	protein, potassium, vitamin E	0.11
Almonds, blanched, slices	2 tbsp	76	1	7	1	protein, vitamin E	0.05
Almonds, dried	1 ounce	164	3	14	1	protein, potassium, vitamin E	0.11
Almonds, dried, chopped	2 tbsp	94	2	8	1	protein, potassium, vitamin E	0.06
Almonds, dried, slices	2 tbsp	69	1	6	0	protein, vitamin E	0.04
Almonds, dried, slivered	2 tbsp	78	2	7	1	protein, vitamin E	0.05
Almonds, dried, whole	2 tbsp	103	2	9	1	protein, potassium, vitamin E	0.07
Almonds, oil roasted	1 ounce	172	3	16	1	protein, potassium, vitamin E	0

Omega-3s (grams)	Amount	Food Item	Calories	Fiber (grams)	Fat (grams)	Saturated Fat (grams)	Good source of:
0.48	1 ounce	Beechnuts, dried	163	1	14	2	protein, potassium, vitamin E
0.94	1 ounce	*Black walnuts, dried (whole, chopped, ground)*	172	1	16	1	protein, potassium, vitamin E
0.52	2 tbsp	Black walnuts, dried and chopped	95	1	9	1	protein
0.33	2 tbsp	Black walnuts, dried and ground	61	1	6	0	protein
0.19	1 ounce	Breadfruit seeds, raw	55	1	2	0	protein, potassium
0.26	one half	Butternut, dried	18	0	2	0	vitamin E
1.31	2 tbsp	Butternuts, dried	92	1	9	0	protein, vitamin E
2.47	1 ounce	*Butternuts, dried*	174	1	16	0	protein, potassium, vitamin E
0.06	2 tbsp	Chestnut Flour	27	N/A	0	0	--
0.23	1 ounce	Chestnut Flour	103	0	1	0	protein, potassium
1.1	1 ounce	*Chia Seeds, dried*	134	7	7	3	protein, potassium
0.18	one half	English walnut halves, dried	13	0	1	0	vitamin E
2.57	1 ounce	*English walnuts, dried (whole, chopped, halves, or ground)*	185	2	18	2	protein, potassium, vitamin E
1.36	2 tbsp	English walnuts, dried, chopped	98	1	10	1	protein
1.14	2 tbsp	English walnuts, dried, halves	82	1	8	1	protein
5.14	1 ounce	*Flaxseed*	140	8	10	1	protein, potassium, vitamin E
3.51	2 tbsp	Flaxseed	95	5	7	1	protein, vitamin E, potassium
0.18	2 tbsp	French bean seeds, dry	79	6	0	0	protein, potassium
0.22	1 ounce	French bean seeds, dried	97	7	1	0	protein, potassium
0.16	2 tbsp	Hickory nuts, dried	99	1	10	1	protein, vitamin E

Omega-3s (grams)	Amount	Food Item	Calories	Fiber (grams)	Fat (grams)	Saturated Fat (grams)	Good source of:
0.3	1 ounce	Hickory nuts, dried	186	2	18	2	protein, potassium, vitamin E
0.28	1 ounce	Pecans, dried (whole, chopped, or halves)	196	3	20	2	protein, potassium, vitamin E
0.15	2 tbsp	Pecans, dried and chopped	103	1	11	1	protein, vitamin E
0.12	2 tbsp	Pecans, dried and ground	82	1	9	1	protein
0.11	2 tbsp	Pine nuts, dried	96	1	9	1	protein, vitamin E, potassium
0.22	1 ounce	Pine nuts, dried	178	3	17	3	protein, potassium, vitamin E
0.12	2 tbsp	Sesame Butter Paste	190	2	16	2	protein, vitamin E, potassium
0.11	1 ounce	Sesame Butter Paste	169	2	14	2	protein, potassium, vitamin E
0.61	2 tbsp	Sesame Seed Salad Dressing	136	0	14	2	potassium, vitamin E
0.61	1 ounce	Sesame Seed Salad Dressing	136	0	14	2	potassium, vitamin E
0.08	2 tbsp	Sesame seeds, dried kernals	110	2	10	1	protein, vitamin E
0.12	1 ounce	Sesame seeds, dried kernels	167	3	16	2	protein, potassium, vitamin E
0.11	1 ounce	Sesame seeds, dried seeds	162	3	14	2	protein, potassium, vitamin E
0.07	2 tbsp	Sesame seeds, dried, whole	103	2	9	1	protein
0.12	2 tbsp	Tahini (from roasted/toasted kernels)	179	3	16	2	protein, vitamin E, potassium
0.12	2 tbsp	Tahini (from unroasted kernels)	170	3	16	2	protein, vitamin E, potassium
0.12	1 ounce	Tahini kernels	169	3	15	2	protein, potassium, vitamin E

Nuts/Nut Butters/Nut Powders*/Nut flours/Seeds—Common Measures* (continued from previous page)

*Negligible source of cholesterol

Oils ❖

You've heard this from me before and you'll hear again and again and again: when it comes to fat, a little dab will do 'ya. The best advice is to REDUCE and SUBSTITUTE. That is, reduce all fat and substitute better ones.

You'll see a form of oil on here that is not terribly high in omega-3s: extra virgin olive oil. I've chosen it as one of my top picks because it has other health benefits, and often provides a flavor you are looking for in a salad or another cold dish.

Omega-3s (grams)	Amount	Food Item	Calories	Fat (grams)	Saturated Fat (grams)	Cholesterol (milligrams)	Good source of:
0.27	2 tbsp	Avocado Oil	248	28	3	– –	– –
	1	California Avocado	306	30	0	3	vitamin E
2.6	2 tbsp	Canola Oil	248	28	2	0	vitamin E
0.45	2 tbsp	Carob Seed Oil	248	28	6	0	– –
5.11	2 tbsp	Cod Liver Oil (Fish Oil)	245	27	6	155	vitamin E
0.19	2 tbsp	Corn Oil (Salad or Cooking)	241	27	3	0	vitamin E
0.19	2 tbsp	Date Pit Oil	248	28	13	0	– –
0.2	2 tbsp	Extra Virgin Olive Oil NOI	252	28	4	– –	vitamin E
4.66	2 tbsp	Fenugreek Seed Oil	248	28	11	0	– –
3.06	2 tbsp	Herring Oil (Fish Oil)	245	27	6	208	vitamin E

Oils* (continued from previous page)

Omega-3s (grams)	Amount	Food Item	Calories	Fat (grams)	Saturated Fat (grams)	Cholesterol (milligrams)	Good source of:
15.04	**2 tbsp**	**Linseed/Flaxseed Oil** *Note: while this is a great source of omega-3s, you would be much better off to use the whole seed, which would help you get more fiber and other phytonutrients.*	239	27	3	--	--
6.32	2 tbsp	Menhaden Fish Oil	245	27	8	142	vitamin E
0.49	2 tbsp	Oat Oil	240	27	5	0	vitamin E
0.16	2 tbsp	Olive Oil (Salad or Cooking)	239	27	4	0	vitamin E
0.44	2 tbsp	Rice Bran Oil	240	27	5	0	vitamin E
0	2 tbsp	Safflower Oil Linoleic (over 70%)	241	27	2	0	vitamin E
8.79	2 tbsp	Salmon Oil (Fish Oil)	245	27	5	132	vitamin E
6.02	2 tbsp	Sardine Oil (Fish Oil)	245	27	8	193	vitamin E
1.4	2 tbsp	Soybean Lecithin Oil	208	27	4	0	vitamin E
0.24	2 tbsp	Sunflower Oil (Linoleic-Hydrogenated)	240	27	4	0	vitamin E
0.19	2 tbsp	Teaseed Oil	240	27	6	0	--
0.63	2 tbsp	Tomatoseed Oil	240	27	5	0	vitamin E
2.83	**2 tbsp**	**Walnut Oil**	241	27	2	0	vitamin E

*Negligible Source of Protein, Fiber, Vitamin C, Folate, and Potassium

Produce*

The more produce you can eat, the better! So don't ignore other produce just because it wasn't one of my top picks.

Omega-3 (grams)	Amount	Food Item	Calories	Fiber (grams)	Good source of:
0.19	2 cups	Arugula, chopped, raw	29	2	folate, potassium
0.09	2 cups	Bibb Lettuce, chopped	15	1	folate, potassium
0.23	2 cups	Broccoli, raw, chopped	49	5	vitamin C, folate, vitamin E, potassium
0.15	2 cups	Cauliflower, raw, chopped	50	5	vitamin C, folate, potassium
0.7	3 ounces	Dried Spirulina Seaweed	247	3	folate, vitamin E, potassium
0.98	1 cup	Dried Spirulina Seaweed	345	4	folate, vitamin E, potassium
0.72	3 ounces	Grape Leaves, canned	59	--	folate
0.73	3 ounces	Grape Leaves, raw, chopped	79	9	folate, vitamin E, potassium
0.12	1 cup	Grape Leaves, raw, chopped	13	2	--
0.73	3 ounces	Grape Leaves, raw (each)	79	9	folate, vitamin E, potassium
0.24	2 cups	Kale, raw, chopped	67	3	vitamin C, folate, potassium
0.01	1/2 cup	Leeks (leaves and bulb), freeze-dried	5	0	--
0.59	3 ounces	Leeks (leaves and bulb), freeze-dried	273	9	vitamin C, folate, vitamin E, potassium
0.02	1 cup	Leeks (leaves and bulb), freeze-dried	10	0	--
0.18	2 cups	Leeks, fresh, chopped (leaves and bulb)	109	3	vitamin C, folate, vitamin E, potassium

Produce* (continued from previous page)

Omega-3 (grams)	Amount	Food Item	Calories	Fiber (grams)	Good source of:
0.85	3 ounces	Mungo beans, dry seeds	290	16	folate, potassium
2.07	*1 cup*	*Mungo beans, dry seeds*	706	38	folate, vitamin E, potassium
–	3 ounces	Purslane, chopped, raw	14	1	potassium
–	1 cup	Purslane, boiled	21	1	potassium
0.61	*2 cups*	*Radish sprouts, raw*	37	2	folate
0.27	1 cup	Radish sprouts, raw	16	1	folate
0.26	*2 cups*	*Raspberries*	121	17	vitamin C, vitamin E, folate, potassium
0.24	*2 cups*	*Strawberries, slices*	91	7	vitamin C, folate, potassium
0.22	*2 cups*	*Strawberries, whole*	86	7	vitamin C, folate, potassium
0.01	2 cups	Swiss chard/sliverbeet, chopped	16	1	vitamin E, potassium

*Negligible Source of Fat, Saturated Fat and Cholesterol

Soy Foods*

There are so many reasons to include soy foods—not just omega-3s. They can help to reduce cholesterol levels, protect against cancer, and control blood sugar levels if you have diabetes. If you're not sure how to use soy foods, be sure and check out the information in Chapter 6 and try the delicious soy recipes in Chapter 8.

Omega-3 (grams)	Amount	Food Item	Weight (grams)	Calories	Fiber (grams)	Fat (grams)	Saturated (grams)	Good source of:
0.34	1 piece	Dried Tofu-Koyadofu- w/Calcium Sulfate	17	82	0	5	1	--
1.72	3 ounces	Dried Tofu-Koyadofu- w/Calcium Sulfate	85	408	1	26	4	--
0.62	1/2 cup	Full Fat Soy Flour, stirred, roasted	43	187	4	9	1	vitamin E, potassium
1.24	3 ounces	Full Fat Soy Flour, stirred, roasted	85	375	8	19	3	vitamin E, potassium, folate
0.62	3 ounces	Natto	85	180	5	9	1	potassium
0.64	1/2 cup	Natto	87	185.5	5	10	1	potassium
0.51	3 ounces	Soybeans, cooked	85.5	147.5	5	8	1	vitamin E, potassium
0.51	1/2 cup	Soybeans, cooked	86	149	5	8	1	vitamin E, potassium
1.13	3 ounces	Soybeans, roasted	85	354	8	17	2	vitamin E, potassium, folate
1.24	1/2 cup	Soybeans, roasted	93	387	9	19	3	vitamin E, potassium, folate
1.23	3 ounces	Soybeans, dry, roasted	85	383	7	18	3	vitamin E, potassium, folate
0.18	1/2 cup	Tempeh	83	160	4	9	2	potassium
0.19	3 ounces	Tempeh	85	164	5	9	2	potassium

Soy Foods* (continued from previous page)

Omega-3 (grams)	Amount	Food Item	Weight (grams)	Calories	Fiber (grams)	Fat (grams)	Saturated (grams)	Good source of:
0.82	1/2 cup	Tofu (prepared with Nigari), fried	61	165	2	12	2	– –
1.15	3 ounces	Tofu (prepared with Nigari), fried	85	230	3	17	2	– –
0.17	1 piece	Tofu w/Calcium Sulfate, fried	13	35	1	3	0	– –
1.14	3 ounces	Tofu w/Calcium Sulfate, fried	85	230	3	17	2	– –
0.34	1 piece	Tofu, dried, frozen	17	82	1	5	1	– –
1.72	*3 ounces*	*Tofu, dried, frozen*	85	408	6	26	4	– –
0.18	1 piece	Tofu, fried	13	35	1	3	0	– –
1.15	3 ounces	Tofu, fried	85	230	3	17	2	– –
0.57	3 ounces	Tofu, hard	85	124	1	9	1	– –
0.81	*1 piece*	*Tofu, hard*	122	178	1	12	1.76	potassium
0.08	1 each	Vegetarian Bacon Strips	5	16	0	1	0.23	– –
0.27	*1 each*	*Vegetarian Sausage Links*	25	64	1	5	0.73	– –
0.41	*1 each*	*Vegetarian Sausage Patties*	38	97	1	7	1.11	vitamin E

*Negligible source of cholesterol, Vitamin C

Grains*

Grains aren't the greatest source of omega-3s, but they are still VERY essential to good health. Try to choose whole grains—not white ones and you'll be far better off nutritionally speaking.

Omega-3 (grams)	Amount	Food Item	Calories	Fiber (grams)	Fat (grams)	Good source of:
0.21	1/4 cup	Wheat germ, raw	103	4	3	protein, folate, potassium, vitamin E
0.23	1/4 cup	Wheat germ, toasted	108	4	3	protein, folate, potassium, vitamin E
0.02	1 cup	White rice, cooked	205	1	0	folate
0.16	1 cup	Wild rice, cooked	166	3	1	protein, potassium

*Negligible saturated fat, cholesterol

Herbs and Spices*

Top Picks from Kris: They're all great! While none of these herbs/spices has a significant amount of omega-3s, they do have some. Every little bit helps! Plus, many of these herbs/spices have important antioxidants that keep omega-3s from oxidizing or becoming rancid (for more on this, see Chapter 6).

Omega-3s (grams)	Amount	Food Item
0.01	1 tsp.	Cayenne Pepper, dried, ground
0.02	1 tsp.	Chili Powder
0.02	1 tsp.	Crumbled Bay Leaf
0.02	1 tsp.	Dried Marjoram
0.01	1 tsp.	Dried Rosemary
0.01	1 tbsp.	Fresh Peppermint
0.01	1 tbsp.	Fresh Rosemary
0.01	1 tbsp.	Fresh Thyme
0.02	1 tsp.	Ground Basil
0.09	1 tsp.	Ground Cloves
0.06	1 tsp.	Ground Oregano
0.01	1 tsp.	Ground Sage
0.05	1 tsp.	Ground Tarragon
0.01	1 tsp.	Ground Thyme
0.01	1 tsp.	Ground Turmeric
0.02	1 tsp.	Paprika
0.01	1 tsp.	Red Pepper, dried, ground
0.01	1 tsp.	Saffron Spice
0.09	1 tsp.	Yellow Mustard Seed

*Negligible fat, saturated fat, cholesterol, and fiber

Legumes*

Like whole grains, legumes aren't necessarily a great source of omega-3s.
But, they're still an awesomely great source of fiber and protein, for very little fat.
So, go ahead and have some meat-free meals with the bean of your choice.

Omega-3 (grams)	Amount	Food Item	Calories	Fiber (grams)	Good source of:
0.22	1 cup	Baked beans, canned, vegetarian	236	13	protein, potassium
0.08	1 cup	Baked beans, canned with pork	268	14	protein, potassium
0.37	1 cup	Baked beans, homemade	382	14	protein, potassium
0.15	1/2 cup	Kidney beans, cooked	112	6	protein, folate, potassium
0.11	1/2 cup	Lupins, cooked	99	2	protein, potassium
0.30	1/2 cup	Mungo beans, cooked	95	7	protein, potassium
0.09	1/2 cup	Pinto beans, cooked	117	7	protein, folate, potassium

* Negligible fat, saturated fat, cholesterol

Chapter 5

Reeling in the Basics: Buying, Storing, and Cooking Fish

If you haven't cooked much fish, you might not know where to start. While we may feel very confident in the kitchen with beef fillets, pasta sauces, or even Indian curries, there is something about being faced with a fish fillet that makes many cooks nervous. Please be assured that there is nothing too difficult about cooking fish, and one of the great benefits for us with our busy lives is that it is so quick. With a piece of tasty, fresh fish and a few cupboard staples or household herbs, such as lemon and parsley, you can have a delicious and healthy meal on the table in just a few minutes. Wondering how? Read on! This chapter contains loads of great advice and handy hints for the novice as well as the experienced fish chef.

First, though, I would like to capture your attention with three key points about fish:

- To preserve the omega-3s, cook fish at lower temperatures or sealed in foil. High cooking temperatures, especially under direct heat, can destroy nearly half the omega-3s in fish.
- If fish smells fishy, you don't want it. Fresh fish should have no odor or should just smell like the sea, a little salty. I'll talk more about finding the freshest fish later in the chapter.
- While many types of fish are high in omega-3s, I recommend that you exercise caution when eating select varieties. There are two main reasons:
  - Some may be too high in cholesterol, which can wreak havoc with your heart health. If you are watching your intake of cholesterol from your diet, which is particularly important if the level of cholesterol in your blood is high,

you can check the amount of cholesterol in different types of fish and other seafood in the charts in Chapter 4. Some seafood, including calamari, caviar, and shrimp, contains higher amounts of cholesterol and should be eaten only about once a week if you have a high blood cholesterol level. These foods, especially caviar, don't tend to be everyday foods in our diet anyway! (You can read a lot more about cholesterol in Chapter 2.)

- Some fish are high in mercury. This topic requires a special discussion to understand the entire perspective. Read on. . . .

Mercury in Fish: Putting it into Perspective

Yes, certain types of fish may contain increased levels of mercury and some other chemicals found in the environment—which means we should all limit how much we eat of these particular types. Pregnant women need to be particularly attentive to limiting such fish intake because it tends to settle in the brain and nervous system of their developing babies, and this has been linked with learning disabilities. The FDA also recommends that nursing mothers and young children also limit the amount they eat of these types of fish.

Fish Facts

If you're pregnant, likely to become pregnant, breastfeeding, or a young child...

The FDA recently issued special guidelines for women who are pregnant, may become pregnant, or are breastfeeding, and young children, regarding the amounts and types of fish they should eat. This is because certain types of fish tend to contain higher amounts of mercury, and this can cause problems for the

(continued on next page)

---

baby's or child's developing nervous system. The types of fish highest in mercury are shark, swordfish, tilefish, and king mackerel, and these should be avoided.

What about other types of fish? The FDA recommends choosing a variety of other fish, and limiting total fish intake to 12 ounces a week. Remember that one serving is generally between 3 and 6 ounces, so this is still two or more healthy fish meals each week.

If not...

If you're not pregnant, likely to become pregnant, nursing, or a young child, the FDA recommends limiting consumption of the fish highest in mercury (shark, swordfish, king mackerel, and tilefish) to 7 ounces each week, and limiting fish containing moderate amounts (fresh tuna, orange roughy, marlin, red snapper) to 14 ounces a week. There aren't any limits placed on other types of fish, but I always feel it is best to go for a variety, rather than large amounts of any one particular type, with all areas of my diet.

What about fish caught by family and friends?

Depending on where the fish is caught, it may be higher in mercury or other chemicals. The Environmental Protection Agency recommends that women who are or may become pregnant or are breastfeeding limit their intake of sport-caught fish to 6 ounces weekly, and that young children consume 2 ounces or less. You can also contact your local or state health or environmental protection department to ask them about the safety of the waterway the fish has been caught from, or check the Environmental Protection Agency's website for advisories in your area on www.epa.gov.

Is there mercury in my mahi-mahi?

You may be wondering how the mercury and other chemicals get into the fish. These chemicals are present at low levels in freshwater streams, lakes, and oceans, either naturally or through pollution. Fish absorb small amounts of the chemicals as they feed, and in the smaller fish the levels generally remain very low. The levels are only thought to become problematic as the bigger fish eat the smaller fish, and the even bigger fish eat those fish, and then the even bigger fish are eaten by the biggest fish. Thus, as the biggest fish eat the smaller fish, and absorb the chemicals from those smaller fish, their levels of the chemicals can build up. That is why it's usually the biggest, fish-eating fish, such as sharks and swordfish, that have the higher chemical levels.

That said, the U.S. Centers for Disease Control and Prevention (CDC) says we should not shy away from all fish because of the fear of mercury. How excessive mercury in fish (note the key word *excessive*) and the health benefits of fish because of omega-3s square off is *"a very difficult message to convey,"* says epidemiologist Tom Sinks of the National Center for Environmental Health, part of the CDC. *"Fish is a vehicle by which people are exposed to mercury. But at the same time, fish is a good source of protein and nutrients, an important part of the diet, and one we want people to eat in a healthy way."*

How much fish can I eat safely?

The best advice is to be aware of fish that tend to be high in mercury, and limit the how much you eat of these particular varieties. The *Fish Facts* sidebar (see p. 76) gives you the recommendations on fish intake from the FDA, both for pregnant and nursing moms and all the rest of us. Note that some health experts are also concerned about pregnant women's intake of tuna, as it is the most popular fish eaten in the USA and may be high in mercury depending on where it comes from. The FDA is investigating the issue of mercury in tuna, but just to be on the safe side, some experts do recommend that women avoid fresh tuna (in other words, tuna that is not canned, such as tuna steaks) while they're pregnant.

Canned tuna is another often-misunderstood topic. Yes, there is concern about eating too much canned tuna, because some of it (again depending on the waters from which it is fished) can be higher in mercury. Just to be on the cautious side, The Washington State Department of Health recently issued the following guidelines about how much canned fish is safe to eat, based on body weight:

Body Weight:	Safe amount of tuna to eat per week:
25 lbs.	1 tablespoon
50 lbs.	2 oz.
75 lbs.	3 oz.
100 lbs.	5 oz.
125 lbs.	1 can or 6 oz.
150 lbs.	1 can or 6 oz.
175 lbs.	9 oz.
200 lbs. or more	10 oz.

Note again a critical perspective: Even within the world of canned tuna, there are tremendous differences. Fortunately, the type of canned fish I want you to eat is one of the lowest in mercury: albacore. Chunk and chunk light varieties are also lower in mercury than other canned varieties, while those that tend to be higher are solid white or chunk white types.

The good news is that following the guidelines still allows plenty of room to choose two heart-healthy servings of fish every week, as recommended by the American Heart Association. And the best news is that some of the fish that is highest in omega-3s, salmon and sardines, are quite low on the mercury scale—so don't worry! Says Tom Sinks of the CDC: *"We want to encourage people not to avoid fish, but to advise them that some fish have higher levels of mercury, and if they're concerned, they should avoid those fish."*

Getting the Most Omega-3s. . . from the Best Fish

If you found the chart in Chapter 4 daunting, then here's a simplified version of knowing where to get the most omega-3s. I've divided up fish into two categories when it comes to reeling in the most omega-3s:

- *Best Catch* (supplies an average of 1.4 grams of omega-3s per 3-ounce serving):
  Most varieties of salmon (except lox and chum)
  Pacific and Jack mackerel
  Whitefish (except smoked)
  Butterfish
  Sablefish
  Atlantic herring
  Sardines
  European anchovies (21 of those little fishies makes a 3-ounce serving)

- *Second choice* (supplies 0.8 to 1.1 grams of omega-3s per 3-ounce serving):
  Atlantic and Spanish mackerel
  Rainbow trout
  Pacific and Eastern oysters
  Striped bass
  Swordfish
  Halibut
  Atlantic and Pacific oysters
  Canned white tuna (albacore)
  Blue fin tuna
  Rainbow smelt
  Chum salmon (canned)

Which salmon?

While all salmon is high in omega-3s, you might want to swim after the richest source: the deeper-colored the salmon, the more omega-3s it contains. Chinook, or king salmon, has the most omega-3s; pink salmon is paler and has less omega-3s; chum is the lowest in omega-3s. Generally, the more expensive the salmon, the more omega-3s it has—you really do get what you pay for in this case. Do note that, if you are buying farmed salmon, the color is not an indicator of the amount of omega-3s it contains as farmed salmon's color changes according to what it is fed.

A note for sardine lovers

Sardine lovers can slide into a few more omega-3s by choosing their tiny fishes wisely—rather, the oil in which the little guys are packed. Depending on the brand, sardines can be packed in olive, cottonseed, soybean, or sardine oil. Of these, only sardine oil contains EPA and DHA, the most valuable omega-3s found in fish. Look for it on the label as "sild oil" or "sild sardine oil."

From the Store to Your Dinner Plate: the Facts on Fish

How to buy fish . . . if it smells fishy walk away!

Odor is your best indicator about the quality of the fish you buy. When you walk into a fish store or approach the fish counter if you're in a supermarket, are you greeted with the crisp clean scent of salt and ice? When you smell your fish, does it smell of nothing at all or a little salty like the sea? This is what you should smell. If the fish smells at all fishy, vaguely foul, or even somewhat less than fresh, something could be amiss. I highly recommend that you walk away and find another fresh fish source.

The look of the fish is also key. If you are *buying whole fish* look for:

- Moist, and even slippery, skin
- A shiny skin with firmly attached scales (if unscaled) and bright coloring
- Bright red, moist gills
- Firm flesh, which bounces back when touched
- Crystal clear eyes—not opaque or sunken into the surrounding skin
- A fresh smell—remember, fresh fish should smell like nothing or simply the sea

If you prefer the convenience of *buying fillets or steaks* look for:

- Firm flesh—run your hand across the top. If the flesh flakes off, the fish has been in the case too long
- Clear white or red color, depending on the variety of fish
- Even coloring
- Moist appearance

How do I store fish?

While it's always best to cook fish the day you buy it, sometimes that's just not possible. To store *fish* for a day or two fresh, try:

- Rinsing when you arrive home, placing in an air/water-tight container and adding ice cubes. If the ice melts, drain and cover with new ice
- Keeping fish in the coldest part of your refrigerator

Store *live clams and mussels* up to two days in the refrigerator by:

- Placing in an open container in a single layer covered with a moist cloth

Shucked clams and mussels store up to three days in the refrigerator when you:

- Place them in a container in their *liquor,* which is the liquid surrounding them.

Frozen fish is just fine, and may be convenient if you need help to eat more fish. Store frozen fish no more than six months, as after that it tends to lose its flavor. Remember never to refreeze thawed fish—you may need to check with your provider that the fish you buy hasn't been frozen and thawed before purchase.

What to do with what fish?

The flesh of fish can be dry or moist, soft or meaty. You'll want to choose the best cooking method for the fillet you choose. Here's a little guidance; you'll see that most fish can be cooked in more than one manner:

Fish to steam or poach:

Bass, flounder, mackerel, mahi-mahi, monkfish, orange roughy, pike, pollack, salmon, grouper, skate, snapper, swordfish, tuna, whitefish

Fish to grill or broil:

Bass, bluefish, butterfish, catfish, cod, flounder, halibut, mackerel, mahi-mahi, mullet, orange roughy, pollack, pompano, sablefish, salmon, shark, skate, snapper, swordfish, trout, tuna, whitefish

Fish to bake:

Bass, bluefish, butterfish, catfish, cod, flounder, halibut, mackerel, mahi-mahi, mullet, orange roughy, pollack, salmon, skate, snapper, swordfish, trout, tuna, whitefish

Fish for making chowder and stews:

Catfish, cod, haddock, halibut, monkfish, orange roughy, pollack

Fish to sauté:

Bass, catfish, flounder, halibut, monkfish, mullet, orange roughy, perch, pollack, salmon, tuna

Fish that benefit from marinating, which compliments strong flavors and moistens the flesh

Mackerel, muskellunge, pickerel, pike, shark, and tuna

Flavors to Compliment Your Fish

Fish goes well with:
► Citrus flavors, especially lemon, lime, and orange
► Garlic
► Ginger
► Green herbs, including parsley, oregano, rosemary, thyme, and cilantro
► Chillies
► Onions and spring onions
► Tomatoes

Cooking secrets

Overcooked fish is chewy and doesn't taste as good. In fact, that's often why people say they don't like fish. Fish cooked for just the right amount of time:

- Should flake easily but shouldn't completely fall apart when you pick it up with a spatula
- Will be opaque almost all the way through, with just the faintest amount of translucency in the middle

Don't forget the age-old "carryover cooking" principle—fish will continue to cook even after you remove it from the heat source, so you'll need to take it off the heat slightly before it's done to prevent overcooking.

My top three methods of cooking fish to preserve the omega-3s *and* to avoid drying it out are baking, poaching, and steaming, but I'll give you tips on sautéing, grilling, and broiling fish as well. For a lot more delicious ideas, take a look at my omega-3-rich fish recipes in Chapter 8.

Baking

My favorite ways of baking fish are two simple ones:

- Bake in a foil packet, with loads of vegetables and seasonings. This is a most "unfussy" and "unmessy" way to cook fish (there are no pots and pans to wash up) and an especially great way to get started down the path of eating more fish. Also, this method conserves omega-3s. Try my Foil-Packet Salmon with Ginger, Spinach, and Carrots to see how delicious baked fish can be.
- Bake fish on a pan, flesh side up (if it has skin). Run a dab of walnut or extra virgin olive oil over the flesh (remember, a little dab will do 'ya) and then season with your favorite herbs. I also like to cover the fish with slices of lime, lemon and/or orange.

Poaching

This gentle cooking method is perfect for seafood, because it imparts lots of moisture and does not mask the delicate flavor of the fish. Traditionally, fish is poached in a court-bouillon—broth made from simmering aromatic vegetables and herbs in water together with peppercorns and something acidic such as lemon juice, vinegar or white wine.

An easier way to poach is to use vegetable or chicken stock, or even a bit of wine. Then,

- Use a pan big enough to lay each piece of fish down flat.
- Pour in enough liquid to just barely cover the fish.
- Bring the liquid to a simmer, and keep it there.
- If you see any bubbles coming up from the bottom of the pan, it's too hot! The ideal poaching temperature is between 165 and 180 degrees F (74 to 82 degrees C).
- Fish that's 1-inch thick will take 15 to 20 minutes; there's no need to flip the fillets during cooking.
- Poached fish will have a very mild, delicate taste, so it's best when served with a flavorful sauce.

Steaming

Steaming is another very gentle cooking method that's especially popular in Asian cuisines for cooking seafood. It's a great way to lock in omega-3s. Here are some tips from the steaming pros:

- Rub the fish with spices, chopped fresh herbs, ginger, garlic or chile peppers to infuse flavor into the flesh while it cooks.
- Use a folding steamer basket (or a bamboo steamer—it might be fun to buy one) with enough room for each piece of fish to lie flat. If you have a wok with a lid and a stand that fits inside it, you may be able to poach fish on a plate on the stand.
- Pour about 1½ inches of water into a pan that fits the steamer; you can throw some more spices or herbs into the water to infuse a little extra subtle flavor.
- Place the steamer over the water, cover the pot, and bring the water to a boil.
- Begin checking the fish for doneness after 10 minutes—try to resist the temptation to take look at the fish otherwise lifting the lid will let the steam out.

Sautéing

The secret to sautéing to both get the omega-3 benefits and keep other fat grams down is to use a good nonstick pan, spray it with no fat cooking spray (such as Pam), and then add just a bit of canola, walnut or extra virgin olive oil. You will often see sauté recipes with *excessive* amounts of oil. Rather than do that, use a dash of oil and then flavor it with highly seasoned broth for extra tasty cooking. You'll love the results! While many recipes call for sautéing at high temperatures, I recommend a gentle, lower temperature sauté to preserve those omega-3s. Also, fish is delicate; it just doesn't need much cooking. Remember these sautéing hints:

- Lay fish in a single layer.
- Flip the fish when it's gently browned on the bottom.
- Continue cooking until it's just about to lose that transparent look in the middle.
- For the best flavor and texture, serve sautéed fish immediately.

Grilling

Grilling fish is challenging because it requires more baby-sitting than other cooking methods. Make a note that grilling can destroy more omega-3s than other cooking methods because you are cooking at such high temperatures. That said, here are a few helpful hints for those rare and special occasions you decide to grill:

- Spray the fish with nonstick cooking spray or brush it very lightly with canola oil.
- Leave the skin on to help retain moisture—even if the skin sticks, you can remove the flesh just fine.
- When the grill is hot and ready, place the fish around the edges of the grill, away from the hottest part of the fire.
- Don't try to lift up the fish right away; it will be stuck to the grill for the first couple of minutes, and prying it up to peek at the underside will tear apart the flesh.

- Once the fish has been on the grill for a couple of minutes it will start to release some of its juices and should no longer be stuck to the grate. Start checking it for color and doneness at this point, and flip it over when it's got light grill marks.
- Remember that fish on the grill requires just a couple of minutes per side, so have the rest of your dinner ready if you choose this cooking style.

Broiling

While broiling is great when you want a fast, simple, hassle-free preparation with delicious results, remember that this high-heat cooking method can destroy more omega-3s than other cooking methods. Consider baking on a rack farther from the heat source. For extra flavor, try rubbing the fish with herbs or spices such as a cajun spice mix before grilling. Fish can also be marinated first. Either buy a commercial marinade or use your imagination.

Enjoying More Fish—for Your Heart and Your Tastebuds

The message from health experts is loud and clear: we need to eat more fish. Don't rely on frozen crumbed and fried fish—they are generally the types with less omega-3s and usually pack a wallop of fat and calories from the crumbing and cooking. Why would you need this type of fast food when fish can be a home-cooked fast food? Fish is naturally low in fat, and the fat it does contain is packed with those valuable, heart-protecting omega-3s. But don't just eat fish because it's healthy; eat fish because it's delicious.

Chapter 6

About Non-Fish Sources of Omega-3s

As you learned in previous chapters, it takes quite a lot of plant-based omega-3s to be equivalent to the more powerful fish-based EPA and DHA. Luckily there are many delicious sources of alpha-linolenic acid, the plant-based omega-3 fat. Some of them may be foods you're not very accustomed to eating or cooking with, so this chapter explains how to choose, store, and cook some of the highest omega-3 foods.

My top picks for non-fish sources of omega-3s are:

- Flaxseed and flaxseed oil
- English walnuts (in measured portions)
- Canola and walnut oil (when you must use oil. . . I'll explain this later in this chapter)
- Greens, greens, and more green vegetables
- Legumes, especially kidney beans, lupins, mungo beans, and pinto beans
- Soy foods

You can also buy "omega-3 eggs" at many supermarkets. There is more information on these eggs in Chapter 4. They are the only vegetarian food that contains some of the fish-type omega-3s, so they may have a place in your diet. However, do be aware that all eggs are rich in cholesterol and may need to be limited if you have a high level of cholesterol in your blood.

Flaxseed

Flaxseed is actually the seed that grows on flax, the same plant from which linen is made. The fat composition of flaxseed is unique; about half of it alpha-linolenic acid, or omega-3 fat.

Not only is flaxseed great for its omega-3 content, but it is also high in soluble fiber—the same type found in oats. While all fiber is beneficial for the body, soluble fiber is thought to be especially helpful in lowering blood cholesterol—helping to stop the artery clogging process—and in keeping blood glucose levels more even in people with diabetes mellitus. Yes, that means that flax has two cholesterol-lowering powers: omega-3s and soluble fiber. There is one other point I want you to remember about the fiber in flaxseed: because the fiber swells up with water to form a type of gel (as you'll see if you put some in a liquid), you need to have plenty of fluids when you eat it. I recommend that you have at least one medium-sized glass of liquid with every tablespoon of flaxseed.

Some of the *many* studies that have shown that eating flaxseed can lower blood cholesterol levels include:

- Total cholesterol levels dropped 9% and LDL (the "bad" cholesterol) decreased 18% when a group of nine healthy women ate 50 grams (about ⅓ cup) of milled flaxseed a day for four weeks (in cereal, smoothies, or baked into breads and muffins) along with their regular diets.
- In a similar study with men and women, 50 grams of flaxseed (eaten daily in muffins) lowered total cholesterol and showed a constant trend of about 11 to 16% lower serum lipids (fat in the blood).

In addition to its rich amounts of omega-3s and soluble fiber, flaxseed is one of the richest sources of lignans, a type of phytochemical (a plant chemical with health benefits) thought to protect against cancer, particularly hormone-sensitive cancers such as those of the breast and prostate. While this is a great advantage to people without these cancers, women who already have breast cancer (and thus possibly men who have prostate cancer) may need to exercise caution before consuming excessive amounts of flaxseeds and oils and should see their physicians before adding flax to their diet.

Buying, storing, and using flaxseed

You can *buy* flaxseed as whole seeds, ground or milled flaxseeds, and flaxseed flour. You may also be able to buy bread baked with flaxseeds. If you are buying whole flaxseeds, look for the split varieties, as splitting the seeds allows the helpful substances to escape from the seeds as they pass through the body. Also, be sure to chew them well. Better still:

- Buy the whole seed, and grind in a coffee grinder
- Buy the ground seeds

Use the flaxseed in:

- Breads and muffins
- Smoothies
- Cold cereal
- Hot cereal
- Yogurt (stir in the split seeds)

Store whole flaxseed or the ground/milled version in the refrigerator or freezer. Why? The omega-3s become rancid—or go "off"—relatively fast, which means they are no good to you.

Walnuts . . . Especially English Ones!

Not all nuts were created equal—especially when it comes to omega-3s. While all walnuts are a good source of omega-3 fats, the English variety is a better source of omega-3s than the black variety. But what if you can't tell the difference in the store? Then just choose any walnuts and enjoy their omega-3 benefits.

As with all nuts, *store* walnuts in the refrigerator or freezer. This prevents the omega-3s from becoming rancid.

Use walnuts however you like them—just sparingly. That's because they are fairly high in fat, and therefore in calories. Yes, all fats, including the healthy ones contain very concentrated calories. Even if you get good amounts of omega-3s in your diet, gaining weight from taking in

Keep Them Cold: Why Omega-3s Feel Happier in the Fridge

You'll see that I recommend you keep many of the plant omega-3s in the refrigerator (of course, the omega-3s in fish should be in the fridge as well!). This is because omega-3 fat is particularly prone to going "off" or becoming rancid. How does this happen? Believe it or not, it's a little like rust forming on a car—both can be caused by a reaction with oxygen, which is why we call this process oxidation. Omega-3 fats are also more likely to become rancid if they are exposed to light. This is a great problem in two respects: firstly the omega-3s lose their health benefits, and secondly rancid fat makes the food taste bad. As some high-omega-3 foods, such as walnut or flaxseed oil, are quite expensive, you don't want to waste them.

Omega-3 foods that are particularly prone to becoming rancid or oxidizing include walnut and flaxseed oil, flaxseeds, and walnuts. Preserve their healthful qualities by:

- ► keeping them in the refrigerator or freezer
- ► keeping them tightly sealed against oxygen in the air
- ► looking for oils sold in dark-colored bottles to protect against light
- ► buying small-sized containers so you use the foods fairly quickly while they're fresh

---

too many calories can *negate* your efforts to eat healthfully. If you are overweight, or are gaining weight and in danger of becoming overweight, you are eating too many calories. Read Chapter 7 to find out whether you fit into these categories and how to eat the appropriate number of calories to keep your weight at a healthy level. If you are watching your calorie intake, use nuts as a garnish or to give crunch to a dish rather than as a frequent snack.

Tasty ideas for using nuts include adding them to cakes and cookies or sprinkling them onto salads, stirfries, desserts, and breakfast cereals to add extra crunch. As well as omega-3s, the nuts provide a protein source (very valuable if you are vegetarian or vegan), fibre, and essential vitamins and minerals.

Choosing the Best Oil . . . When You Need One

If you're *buying* an oil for its omega-3s, canola and walnut oils are two of the best, with just slight differences in their omega-3 content. Flaxseed oil is highest in omega-3s, however its use in the kitchen is limited, as you'll see below. For general cooking, olive oil is another "healthy" oil, though it is not so high in omega-3s. Soybean and peanut oil are also quite good choices. If you're looking for a margarine, try to get one based on these healthier types of oil and avoid any that contain trans fats (which you'll read about in the next chapter).

While we know which oils supply the most omega-3s, that doesn't tell us how to *use* each oil. The most important point is that you cannot cook with flaxseed oil—its healthful qualities are destroyed if it is heated. The best use for flaxseed oil is for drizzling over dishes such as salads. You can experiment by mixing it into different salad dressings. Walnut oil and extra-virgin olive oil are also ideal for salad dressings as they add a delicious flavor. Walnut oil will also add a lovely nutty taste if used in dishes such as grilled fish, whereas canola oil is the one to use if you don't want to add any flavor; it is very bland. While olive oil can be used for gentle sautéing, it is not suitable for frying at very high temperatures. Canola, peanut, or soybean oil would be better choices, though please remember that frying food in oil will make it higher in fat.

The world of oils and margarines is a most confusing one. When you use a healthy one . . . does that mean that you can pour it on? One would almost think so, but the answer is an absolute *no!*

The best advice when it comes to oils and margarines is:

- Reduce the total amount you use in your diet
- Substitute healthier fats when you must use fat.

Don't forget that one tablespoon of either canola or walnut oil (or of any type of oil, for that matter) has a hefty 120 calories. Thus, when you use any oil, always measure carefully. As experienced as I am in the kitchen, I still cannot "eyeball" the amount of oil I need. I once tried to pour in one tablespoon, just to see how I did. I then measured—and found out that I had poured in no less than one-quarter cup—or 480 calories!

Be sure to *store* the omega-3 oils (as well as olive oil) in the refrigerator to preserve those healthy fats.

How to Buy, Store, and Cook Arugula, Other Greens, Broccoli, and Other Vegetables

These green vegetables are not a huge source of omega-3s, however they do contain significant amounts. And because we eat vegetables everyday (or we should be, in any case), their omega-3s do add up and become quite valuable. While some of the vegetables I discuss, such as broccoli, will be very familiar, you may find others a little more unusual.

Arugula

The delicious green leaves of this peppery-flavored vegetable can be found in most supermarkets now, and almost always in health food stores. When *buying* arugula, choose leaves that are bright green and fresh looking. To *store* it, wrap the arugula in a damp paper towel and place it in a vented container (such as an open plastic bag). Arugula is best if used within two days after purchase. *Use* it in salads, soups, and sautéed vegetable dishes. *Growing* arugula is very easy, so give it a try during the gardening seasoning.

Spinach

This vitamin-rich leafy vegetable can be purchased fresh year round; frozen is another great alternative (I prefer that you don't go for canned spinach, as it tends to be higher in salt). When *buying* fresh spinach, choose leaves that are crisp and dark green with a nice fresh fragrance. Depending on the variety, the leaves may be either curled or smooth. Avoid leaves that are limp, damaged, or discolored. Don't hesitate to buy spinach bagged ready for use (usually found with the bagged salads). To *store* spinach, rinse the leaves in cool water and dry on paper toweling. Wrap leaves tightly in plastic or a zip lock bag and refrigerate. Note that you don't have to go to this trouble with the bagged, ready-washed spinach. In any case, this vegetable will taste better and retain more nutrients if used within three days. U*se* raw spinach in salads or cook it (usually by boiling or sautéing) and use it as a vegetable or part of a dish. Try mixing some in to your next stir-fry just before you take it off the heat.

Kale

This leafy green has a mild cabbage flavor and comes in many varieties and colors. The colors of the leaves are deep green and variously tinged with shades of blue or purple. This leafy green is officially "in season" in the winter months, but tends to be available year-round. To *buy* kale, choose leaves that are crisp and fresh and have a deep color with no yellow tinge. *Store* kale in dry plastic bags in the refrigerator for up to three days. When *using* kale keep in mind the following: smaller leaves have a milder flavor; they can be cooked whole and often have stems tender enough to eat. With larger leaves, you'll need to cut out and discard the stems and then chop the leaves into small pieces. Kale can be cooked in any way suitable for spinach and is also delicious in soups. The smaller, more tender leaves make a great addition to salads.

Grape leaves

This more unusual vegetable is not usually available in the grocery fresh, so look for canned grape leaves packed in brine. *Store* them in your pantry until you are ready to use them. Rinse them well before using, to remove some of the salty flavor and sodium content. If you find and buy fresh grape leaves, store them in your refrigerator for up to a few days. To cook them, simmer in water for about ten minutes to soften them enough to be pliable. *Use* grape leaves to wrap foods, as in Greek dolmathes, or as garnishes, decorations, or in salads. You may see them as an ingredient in a Greek cookbook.

Broccoli

Broccoli is available year-round, with a peak season from October through April. This deep emerald-green vegetable (which sometimes has a purple tinge) comes in tight clusters of tiny buds that sit on stout, edible stems. When *buying* broccoli, look for a deep, strong green, or green and purple color; the buds should be tightly closed and the leaves crisp. Don't hesitate to buy broccoli florets ready to use in bags; frozen broccoli is also an excellent alternative with fabulous nutritional value. To *store* fresh broccoli refrigerate it unwashed, in an airtight bag, for up to four days. When using broccoli, peel the stalks before cooking if they are tough.

Leeks

This vegetable is available year-round in most regions. The leek, which is related to garlic and onions, has thick, white stalks that are cylindrical in shape and have a slightly bulbous root end. Leeks have broad, flat, dark green leaves that wrap tightly around each other like a rolled newspaper. When *buying* leeks, choose ones with crisp, brightly colored leaves and an unblemished white portion; avoid any with withered or yellow-spotted leaves. To *store* leeks refrigerate them in a plastic bag for up to five days. When using leeks be sure to wash them thoroughly to remove grit and sand, which accumulates under the outer layers of the leaves. It is sometimes easiest to split the leek in half lengthwise to make sure you've removed all the grit. Leeks are then ready for use and can be cooked whole as a vegetable or chopped and used in salads, soups, and in a multitude of other dishes. Cooking time will vary according to the leek's size; when you can pierce the base easily with a knife, the leeks are ready. Avoid overcooking, which will makes leeks tough.

Help with Buying, Cooking, and Storing Legumes

Hopefully you'll try all the dried bean and pea—alias legumes—recipes in this book. Better yet, I hope that legumes will become your main protein source for at least one lunch and dinner during the week, preferably even more. They are not just a good source of omega-3s, they have a whole range of nutritional benefits. They are an extremely important source of protein (especially for vegetarians), a great source of many vitamins and minerals, and contain soluble fibre. We read about this earlier when I was discussing flaxseeds; you'll remember that soluble fibre helped to lower cholesterol levels and keep blood glucose levels more even in people with diabetes.

You can *buy* many types of legumes either dried or in cans. While the canned varieties are undoubtedly more convenient, it is more economical to buy them in dried form. Some of the more uncommon legumes are only available dried. You'll find helpful advice for cooking dried legumes below. These can be added to soups, stews, and salads. By adding beans to dishes such as chili con carne, less meat is used and the meal becomes healthier, with less fat and more fibre. Also try recipes for dips such as hummus and white bean paste, which make tasty spreads for sandwiches.

You may see a few types of legumes mentioned that are new to you, and I wholeheartedly encourage you to try them. Mungo beans are one less common variety of legume. Please note that they are different from mung beans. Another is lupins. Although these legumes have only recently been grown for commercial sale, lupin seed has been used as a food since ancient times. The Mediterranean white lupin (*Lupinus albus*) has been used as a subsistence crop for three thousand years or more, and the pearl lupin (*L. mutabilis* Sweet) has been cultivated for thousands of years in the Andean Highlands of South America.

Shopping List for Omega-3 Pantry Essentials

These pantry staples will help you to maximize your omega-3 intake:

- ► Omega-3-rich cooking oils: canola and soybean oils
- ► Omega-3-rich oils for use in salads and for drizzling: walnut oil and flaxseed oil (remember to keep flaxseeds and their oil in the refrigerator)
- ► Flaxseeds (split), ground or milled flaxseeds, and flaxseed flour
- ► Walnuts, especially English walnuts (store them in the r efrigerator or freezer for maximum freshness)
- ► Canned grape leaves
- ► Frozen broccoli
- ► Dried or canned legumes, such as lentils, split peas, chickpeas, and kidney beans
- ► Frozen edamame beans
- ► Soy flour, soybeans, soynuts, and soynut butter
- ► Soymilk or soy yogurt
- ► Tofu products and tempeh
- ► Soy-based meat alternatives—frozen, dried, or canned (be sure to choose those with a lower fat content)

How to cook legumes

This guide tells how much water to use per cup of dried legumes, as well as how long to cook them for and the final yield. Please note that you can cook up large batches of legumes and freeze them in individual portions. I suggest freezing them in ½ cup amounts so that you don't have to remember how much is in each packet. They keep in the freezer, when sealed well, for up to six months.

Legume	Water	Cooking Time	Yield
Black beans	4 cups	1½ hours	2 cups
Black-eyed peas	3 cups	1 hour	2 cups
Chick peas (garbanzo beans)	4 cups	3 hours	2 cups
Great Northern beans	3½ cups	3 hours	2 cups
Kidney beans	3 cups	1½ hours	2 cups
Lentils	3 cups	45 minutes	2¼ cups
Lupins	4 cups	45 min–1 hour	2 cups
Mungo beans	2½ cups	1 hour	2 cups
Navy beans	3 cups	2½ hours	2 cups
Pinto beans	3 cups	2½ hours	2 cups
Soy beans	4 cups	3+ hours	2 cups
Split peas	3 cups	45 minutes	2¼ cups

How to Buy, Store, and Cook Soy Foods

I'm very enthusiastic about everyone eating more soy foods—for many, many good health reasons besides their excellent omega-3 content. Like other legumes, they contain soluble fibre and thus can be helpful if you have diabetes or high cholesterol levels. They also contain natural chemicals called phytoestrogens that mimic estrogen in the body and can help to alleviate the symptoms of menopause and protect against breast cancer. However, as with flaxseeds, women who have breast cancer should consult their physician before including very large amounts of soy in their diet.

Soy foods, like some of the other omega-3 rich foods, are unfamiliar to many people. In case you haven't yet discovered this diverse group of ingredients, let's venture into soy foods and their many different forms.

Green vegetable soybeans (edamame)

These large soybeans are harvested when the beans are still green and sweet tasting and can be served as a main dish hot or cold, or even as a snack, after boiling for 15-20 minutes. Edamame is found in most grocery stores fresh in the pod or frozen out of the pod.

Meat alternatives (often called meat analogs)

Meat alternatives made from soybeans contain soy protein or tofu and other ingredients mixed together to simulate various kinds of meat, such as burger, hot dogs, sausages, and bacon. These meat alternatives are sold as frozen, canned, or dried foods. Usually, they can be used the same way as the foods they replace. With so many different meat alternatives available to consumers, the nutritional value of these foods varies considerably. Generally, they are lower in fat, but read the label to be certain.

Miso

Miso is a rich, salty condiment that characterizes the essence of Japanese cooking. The Japanese make miso soup and use it to flavor a variety of foods. A smooth paste, miso is made from soybeans and a grain such as rice, plus salt and a mold culture, and then aged in cedar vats for one to three years. Miso should be refrigerated. Use it to make soup, to which you can add small pieces of tofu and veggies to complete the meal.

Soy flour

Soy flour is made from roasted soybeans ground into a fine powder. All soy flour gives a protein boost to recipes, which can be particularly valuable if you are vegetarian or vegan. Although used mainly by the food industry, soy flour can be found in natural foods stores and some supermarkets. Soy flour is gluten-free, so yeast-raised breads made with soy flour are more dense in texture. Replace ¼ to ⅓ the flour with soy flour in recipes for muffins, cakes, cookies, pancakes, and quick breads.

Soy yogurt

Soy yogurt is made from soymilk. Its creamy texture makes it an easy substitute for cream, sour cream, or cream cheese in meals and recipes. Soy yogurt can be found in a variety of flavors in most grocery stores and also in health food stores. Look for the ones that have been fortified with calcium and extra vitamins.

Soybeans

As soybeans mature in the pod they ripen into a hard, dry bean. Most soybeans are yellow. However, there are brown and black varieties. Whole soybeans (an excellent source of protein and dietary fiber) can be cooked and used in sauces, stews, and soups, and as the main topping for salads.

Soynuts

Roasted soynuts are whole soybeans that have been soaked in water and then baked until browned. Soynuts can be found in a variety of flavors, including chocolate-covered (of course, these are not the most healthful choice!). High in protein and many other nutrients, soynuts are similar in texture and flavor to peanuts. Add them to salads, stir-fries, and breakfast cereal for extra crunch. You can find roasted soynuts in most grocery stores now, and also in health food stores.

Soymilk or soy beverages

Soybeans are soaked, ground fine, and strained to produce a fluid called soy-bean milk, which is a good substitute for cow's milk. Look for calcium- and vitamin-fortified, and reduced-fat soymilk, either plain, vanilla, or chocolate flavored. I find that a large glass of chocolate soymilk satisfies my craving for chocolate!

Tofu and tofu products

Tofu, also known as soybean curd, is a soft cheese-like food made by curdling fresh hot soymilk. Tofu is rich in high-quality protein and B-vitamins, and low in sodium. Firm tofu is dense and solid and can be cubed and served in soups, stir fried, or grilled. Firm tofu is higher in protein, fat, and calcium than other forms of tofu. Soft tofu is good for recipes that call for blended tofu. Silken tofu is a creamy product and can be used as a replacement for sour cream in many dip recipes or pureed for use in creamy dressings. Look for reduced-fat versions of tofu to get the most benefit from it.

Tofu is a bland product that easily absorbs the flavors of other ingredients with which it is cooked. You can add extra flavor by marinading the tofu, and can also buy ready-marinated tofu in many supermarkets and health-food stores. These make especially delicious stir-fries.

Soynut butter

This nutritious spread is made from roasted whole soynuts, which are then crushed and blended with soyoil and other ingredients. Soynut butter has a slightly nutty taste, significantly less fat than peanut butter, and provides all the other benefits of soy.

Tempeh

Tempeh, a traditional Indonesian food, is a chunky, tender soybean cake. Whole soybeans, sometimes mixed with a grain such as rice, are fermented into a rich cake of soybeans with a smoky or nutty flavor. Tempeh slices up similarly to meat and chicken, so can be used in any stir-fry recipe that calls for either one of those. Tempeh can be marinated and grilled and added to soups, casseroles, and chili, or used to make tacos or burgers. While tempeh is an excellent meat replacement, it is not terribly high in omega-3s.

Omega-3 Fats—So Much More than Fish

I am always amazed at the sheer range and variety of foods that contain omega-3s. Whether or not you eat fish, there are plant sources of this health-giving, heart-protecting fat to please every palate. As you've seen in this chapter, it is truly possible to eat these foods at breakfast, lunch, and dinner every day (and if you aren't a fish eater, you will probably need to include them in one more meal each day to meet your requirements of this essential nutrient). I hope you'll try some of my recipes for these foods in Chapter 8, and then try experimenting with your own creations and combinations.

Chapter 7

A Perspective on Omega-3s—the Whole Picture of a Healthy Lifestyle

While omega-3s are a big help—no, a huge one—in helping you fight heart disease, cancer, and autoimmune diseases such as lupus and asthma, they cannot take care of you alone. Indeed, you have to take charge of your health in every way you can.

For example, if you eat three fish dinners per week (or the equivalent in plant foods high in omega-3s), but have fast-food cheeseburgers and fries for lunch a couple of times per week and munch on potato chips as snacks, you basically negate all of those great omega-3s. Similarly, if you don't eat enough fruits and vegetables with all of their beneficial health-protection ingredients you're wasting some of the omega-3s that you worked so hard to get.

My message here is that your whole diet is important, not to mention taking care of your body with exercise. This may seem like hard work, and you may wonder how you can follow the right diet for your individual health status. Maybe you have diabetes, heart disease, or high blood pressure, or worry about developing cancer because others in your family already have. Even more difficult, what should you eat if you have two conditions, such as heart disease and diabetes? Well, here's the good news: the same basic diet is right for just about everyone. Yes, the same great eating style that helps control high blood pressure, for example, will reduce your risk of developing cancer, heart disease, or diabetes. Certainly, there are a few special considerations if you have, for example, diabetes or a high cholesterol level; however, on the whole the guidelines are the same.

I'll begin this chapter by giving you the whole picture of a healthy lifestyle. This gives you the tools to craft a diet for you and your family to:

- control your weight
- reduce the risk of developing problems such as heart disease and some cancers
- help you to combat problems such as diabetes or high blood pressure if you already have them

Then I'll go through a number of all-too-common disorders, including heart disease, high blood pressure, type 2 diabetes, and cancer, and emphasize certain areas of the diet that are most important in the control or prevention of these problems. Of course, having read most of this book by now, you'll remember how important the omega-3s are in all these health conditions.

A Healthy Diet for a Healthy Life

Body weight: keep it lean

Heart disease experts tell us that just carrying around excess baggage can raise cholesterol levels. We also know that being too heavy raises the chance of having high blood pressure, which in turn increases the risk that artery-clogging heart disease will develop. Being overweight also raises the likelihood of developing type 2 diabetes and certain types of cancer. With all these facts in front of us, it makes reducing our weight a national priority. Too many Americans are too heavy and it is, quite literally, killing us. The problem is that it is difficult to lose weight, and easy to become discouraged. Work as many as possible of the healthy diet and lifestyle tips I've listed below into your daily life. Every one of them will help you to meet your weight control goals.

The first step is to figure out what is a healthy weight for you. An easy way is to use a tool called Body Mass Index (BMI). Body mass index is a way that scientists relate your weight to your height, and is

Body Mass Table Index

Body Weight (pounds)

BMI	Normal						Overweight					Obese										Extreme Obesity														
Height (inches)	19	20	21	22	23	24	25	26	27	28	29	30	31	32	33	34	35	36	37	38	39	40	41	42	43	44	45	46	47	48	49	50	51	52	53	54
58	91	96	100	105	110	115	119	124	129	134	138	143	148	153	158	162	167	172	177	181	186	191	196	201	205	210	215	220	224	229	234	239	244	248	253	258
59	94	99	104	109	114	119	124	128	133	138	143	148	153	158	163	168	173	178	183	188	193	198	203	208	212	217	222	227	232	237	242	247	252	257	262	267
60	97	102	107	112	118	123	128	133	138	143	148	153	158	163	168	174	179	184	189	194	199	204	209	215	220	225	230	235	240	245	250	255	261	266	271	276
61	100	106	111	116	122	127	132	137	143	148	153	158	164	169	174	180	185	190	195	201	206	211	217	222	227	232	238	243	248	254	259	264	269	275	280	285
62	104	109	115	120	126	131	136	142	147	153	158	164	169	175	180	186	191	196	202	207	213	218	224	229	235	240	246	251	256	262	267	273	278	284	289	295
63	107	113	118	124	130	135	141	146	152	158	163	169	175	180	186	191	197	203	208	214	220	225	231	237	242	248	254	259	265	270	278	282	287	293	299	304
64	110	116	122	128	134	140	145	151	157	163	169	174	180	186	192	197	204	209	215	221	227	232	238	244	250	256	262	267	273	279	285	291	296	302	308	314
65	114	120	126	132	138	144	150	156	162	168	174	180	186	192	198	204	210	216	222	228	234	240	246	252	258	264	270	276	282	288	294	300	306	312	318	324
66	118	124	130	136	142	148	155	161	167	173	179	186	192	198	204	210	216	223	229	235	241	247	253	260	266	272	278	284	291	297	303	309	315	322	328	334
67	121	127	134	140	146	153	159	166	172	178	185	191	198	204	211	217	223	230	236	242	249	255	261	268	274	280	287	293	299	306	312	319	325	331	338	344
68	125	131	138	144	151	158	164	171	177	184	190	197	203	210	216	223	230	236	243	249	256	262	269	276	282	289	295	302	308	315	322	328	335	341	348	354
69	128	135	142	149	155	162	169	176	182	189	196	203	209	216	223	230	236	243	250	257	263	270	277	284	291	297	304	311	318	324	331	338	345	351	358	365
70	132	139	146	153	160	167	174	181	188	195	202	209	216	222	229	236	243	250	257	264	271	278	285	292	299	306	313	320	327	334	341	348	355	362	369	376
71	136	143	150	157	165	172	179	186	193	200	208	215	222	229	236	243	250	257	265	272	279	286	293	301	308	315	322	329	338	343	351	358	365	372	379	386
72	140	147	154	162	169	177	184	191	199	206	213	221	228	235	242	250	258	265	272	279	287	294	302	309	316	324	331	338	346	353	361	368	375	383	390	397
73	144	151	159	166	174	182	189	197	204	212	219	227	235	242	250	257	265	272	280	288	295	302	310	318	325	333	340	348	355	363	371	378	386	393	401	408
74	148	155	163	171	179	186	194	202	210	218	225	233	241	249	256	264	272	280	287	295	303	311	319	326	334	342	350	358	365	373	381	389	396	404	412	420
75	152	160	168	176	184	192	200	208	216	224	232	240	248	256	264	272	279	287	295	303	311	319	327	335	343	351	359	367	375	383	391	399	407	415	423	431
76	156	164	172	180	189	197	205	213	221	230	238	246	254	263	271	279	287	295	304	312	320	328	336	344	353	361	369	377	385	394	402	410	418	426	435	443

Source: Adapted from Clinical Guidelines on the Identification, Evaluation, and Treatment of Overweight and Obesity in Adults: The Evidence Report

also an indicator of your long-term risk of developing problems such as heart disease and type 2 diabetes. You should aim for a BMI of below 25. As body mass index creeps over 25, it indicates that you are overweight and your health risks increase. To determine your BMI, use the table in this chapter. You will need to know your height and current weight. Please note that this table is only suitable for calculating BMI for adults, and not for anyone under 18 years old.

Using the table, you can also look at your "healthy weight range," or the body weight range that would give you a BMI of 20 to 25. If you are not too far above this range, somewhere within the "healthy weight range" is a good weight to aim for. If you are a long way above the range, just aim to lose a smaller amount of weight, say 10 or 15 pounds, and then either take a break and maintain that lower weight, or set yourself another manageable weight loss goal. No matter how overweight you are, just losing 10 or 20 pounds can bring permanent benefits to your long-term health.

Think Low Fat

There are two main reasons for this guideline: firstly, fats are the most concentrated source of calories in our diet. A teaspoon of butter has more than twice the calories of a teaspoon of sugar. Thus, this is the nutrient most likely to make us gain excess weight. Second, some types of fats tend to raise our cholesterol levels, increasing our risk of a heart attack or stroke.

I recommend that you limit total dietary fat to 20 to 25% of your daily calories. Note that this is less than the latest official guideline, which says it's okay to let total fat go all the way up to 35%. However, we tend to eat a much higher proportion of our fat as omega-6s than as omega-3s. Thus it's hard to eat 35% of our calories as fat and still keep omega-6s at no more than four times the omega-3s in your diet. Most of us tend to eat a diet containing significantly more than 35% of our calories as fat, so you may like to cut down to 35% first and then aim to go lower. Check out the *How Low Can You Go?: Tips on Choosing a Low-Fat Diet* sidebar for more information, and use the following table to ballpark your fat maximum, whatever level you choose.

Calorie level	20% of calories as fat	25% of calories as fat	35% of calories as fat
1500	300 calories; 33 fat grams	375 calories; 42 fat grams	525 calories; 58 fat grams
1600	320 calories; 36 fat grams	400 calories; 44 fat grams	560 calories; 62 fat grams
1700	340 calories; 38 fat grams	425 calories; 47 fat grams	595 calories; 66 fat grams
1800	360 calories; 40 fat grams	450 calories; 50 fat grams	630 calories; 70 fat grams
1900	380 calories; 42 fat grams	475 calories; 53 fat grams	665 calories; 74 fat grams
2000	400 calories; 44 fat grams	500 calories; 56 fat grams	700 calories; 78 fat grams
2100	420 calories; 47 fat grams	525 calories; 58 fat grams	735 calories; 82 fat grams
2200	440 calories; 49 fat grams	550 calories; 61 fat grams	770 calories; 86 fat grams

When you must use fat, make sure it's a healthier type. The best bets for your heart, your cholesterol levels, and your ratio of omega-3 to omega-6 fats are monounsaturated fats and omega-3 fat sources. Read the section on heart disease in this chapter and check back to Chapter 2 for more information on the different types of fat.

Don't eat too much sugar

While fatty foods are the biggest culprit when it comes to gaining excess pounds, large amounts of sugary food can also be a factor. That's not to say that sweet foods should be avoided altogether, it's fine to have the occasional piece of candy or a few teaspoons of sugar each day in tea or coffee. The main problem is large amounts of sugary soda, as each glass can contain about seven teaspoons of sugar. If you do like these drinks, choose the "diet" varieties to avoid the extra calories.

Boost Your Intake of Fruits and Vegetables

The recommended intake of fruit and vegetables is five servings of each per day. If you currently eat less, that would be a great point to aim for. However, if you can, try for a minimum of five serves of fruit *and* five vegetable serves on most days. Yes, this sounds like a lot, but these foods are full of healthy fiber, are packed with vitamins, minerals,

How Low Can You Go? Tips on Choosing a Low-fat Diet

It's helpful to remember where fat tends to be found in the diet. Fruits and vegetables, apart from avocado, do not contain fat. Plain grain foods, such as bread, rice, and pasta tend to be virtually fat-free. Fats are found in meats and dairy foods, cooking oils, margarine and butter, and many processed foods. Here are some ideas to help you reduce your fat intake:

- Cooking food by baking, grilling, broiling, steaming, microwaving, and boiling use less fat than frying.
- Use a minimum amount of oil to cook with, or try using a non-stick pan or substituting a little wine or stock.
- Use little or no margarine or butter.
- Limit your intake of fatty mayonnaise, salad dressings, cream, and full fat sour cream. Reduced-fat or fat free versions of many of these products are available.
- Trim the fat from meat and the skin from chicken. Limit your intake of high-fat meats such as bacon and sausages
- Choose low-fat or fat-free dairy foods such as fat-free or 1% milk and low-fat cheese.
- Read the labels on processed foods to choose lower-fat versions. Keep in mind that processed foods such as cakes and cookies, chocolate, potato chips, and fast-food meals tend to be high in fat.

and other nutrients that are either essential or extremely beneficial to our bodies, and contain no fat (except for avocados).

The "other nutrients" found in fruit and vegetables, often called phytochemicals (meaning plant chemicals), have a variety of beneficial effects in the body, and many are thought to reduce our risk of developing cancer and heart disease. Some do this by preventing the "oxidation" I mentioned earlier in the book, the process that makes omega-3 fats rancid and rusts our car. Believe it or not, a similar process also goes on in our body; among other dangerous effects, it can increase our risk of heart attacks. How can we make sure we eat enough of these precious nutrients? By eating plenty of fruit and vegetables and choosing a rainbow of colors and types. Aim to have green vegetables; red, yellow or orange vegetables; and several different types of fruit every day. This great intake of "anti-oxidants" will also help to preserve the omega-3 fats and allow them to do the best job inside our bodies.

Base each meal around wholegrain cereals, breads, and potatoes

The starchy grain foods and potatoes provide the fuel for our body to function every day, giving us the energy to get out of bed, do the housework, go to work, even just to keep our hearts beating. Thus we should eat these foods, such as breakfast cereal, rice, bread, pasta, or potatoes, at each meal. To make the best choices for your body:

- Be sure to choose low-fat options. On their own, the grain foods and potatoes are very low in fat. Watch out for more processed and higher fat varieties such as croissants, cookies, and french fries.
- Avoid adding fat to these foods. For example, put fat-free sour cream rather than butter on a baked potato, and use the minimum amount of margarine on bread, or even none at all.
- Think high fiber by:
  - Choosing 12-grain bread or oat bran instead of white
  - Change white rice to brown
  - Reach for a high fiber, wholegrain breakfast cereal instead of a higher sugar, refined one
- Try at least one different grain for dinner each week, such as barley, millet, or quinoa

Diversify your protein sources

The main sources of protein in most people's diet are chicken or turkey, beef, and pork. Because these foods can contain significant amounts of fat, our protein intake is closely tied to our fat intake. Rather than rotating between chicken or turkey and beef and pork:

- Include at least two to three fish meals per week
- Enjoy at least one non-meat dinner weekly (yes, that means vegetarian)—more is better. Experiment with vege-burgers or a marinated tofu stir-fry.
- Choose vegetarian or fish sources of protein for several—if not all—lunches each week.
- Bounce in at least one-half cup of beans to your eating plan each week. Try split pea soup, black bean soup, or garbanzo beans instead of chicken on your salad.

Eat a variety of foods high in fiber

In coloring your diet with fruits, vegetables, whole grains, and legumes, you'll be boosting your fiber intake. There are two different types of fiber to look for, with very different benefits for your body:

- Soluble fiber helps to reduce cholesterol levels and evens out blood sugar levels if you have diabetes. Great sources include:
  - Oats and oat bran
  - Legumes, such as lentils, black beans, split peas
  - Barley
  - Flaxseed
  - Fruit and vegetables
- Insoluble fiber is the type that keeps you "regular." Wholewheat foods, such as wholemeal or 12-grain bread and wholegrain breakfast cereals are great sources. Having plenty of fluids will help the fiber to do its job—aim for at least eight glasses daily.

Go easy on the alcohol

As well as the excess calories, which can contribute to gaining excess pounds, drinking too much alcohol can damage our body in many ways. For example, it can lead to liver damage, and tends to raise triglyceride levels in susceptible people. Turn back to Chapter 2 if you want to read more about triglycerides.

The recommended maximum level of alcohol intake is no more than one alcoholic drink each day if you are a woman or for anyone over the age of 65. If you are a man aged up to 65, the level is two drinks daily. A "drink" is a 12-ounce bottle of beer or wine cooler, a 5-ounce glass of wine, or a 1.5 ounce measure of spirits.

Exercise

Indulge your body in daily activity. New guidelines suggest that you need 30 to 60 minutes of activity most—if not every—day of the week. If that's more than you can manage, just aim to do a little more tomorrow than you have done today, and build up from there. If you haven't exercised for a long time or have a health condition, be sure to consult your doctor before you start. And remember that exercise doesn't have to be at the gym. Just gardening or vacuuming, or something as fun as dancing, can be exercise. You simply need to increase your heart rate enough that you are breathing a little harder than usual, but not puffing so hard that you can't say hello to your neighbor comfortably as you stride past.

Needing motivation? Well, just think of the heart as the muscular pump it is. Like all our other muscles, the heart simply cannot be as strong as it needs to be without adequate exercise. If just getting up and strolling around exercises the heart muscle, and all your other muscles, imagine what a brisk walk or spin on the exercise bicycle can do for your body!

Special Tips for Heart Disease

I said it at the beginning of this chapter and I'll say it again—following the healthy diet and lifestyle advice above will help you to control your weight and reduce your risk of developing a host of health problems, including heart disease. It can also assist you in combatting heart disease if you are unfortunate enough to already have it. But there are a few other factors to keep in mind when it comes to this particular health issue. You already know how important the omega-3 fats are in protecting your heart. If you've forgotten the details, have another look at Chapter 2. Likewise, taking the following nutrition tips to heart can help to protect you against the ravages of heart disease.

Watch your saturated and trans fat intake

Keep the lid on saturated fat, the single worst culprit in raising blood cholesterol levels, especially the LDL, the bad cholesterol. You recognize saturated fat, for example, as the white, hard fat that forms on the roast beef platter as it cools. Indeed, all saturated fats are solid at room temperature. In contrast, the other two types of fat, polyunsaturated and monounsaturated, are liquid at room temperature. As you read in Chapter 2, saturated fats are found in animal foods, meats, and dairy food, as well as processed foods containing animal fats or palm or coconut oil.

Also watch out for the dangerous trans fats, which act to raise LDL-cholesterol levels in the same way as saturated fat. Not sure where to find trans fat? Check out the *I Spy: Finding the Trans Fats in Your Diet* sidebar.

Count a maximum of 10% of your calories as saturated or trans fat—better to stop at 7%. Use the following table as a guide:

Calorie level	7% of calories as saturated fat	10% of calories as saturated fat
1500	105 calories; 12 fat grams	150 calories; 17 fat grams
1600	112 calories; 12 fat grams	160 calories; 18 fat grams
1700	119 calories; 13 fat grams	170 calories; 19 fat grams
1800	126 calories; 14 fat grams	180 calories; 20 fat grams
1900	133 calories; 15 fat grams	190 calories; 21 fat grams
2000	140 calories; 16 fat grams	200 calories; 22 fat grams
2100	147 calories; 16 fat grams	210 calories; 23 fat grams
2200	154 calories; 17 fat grams	220 calories; 24 fat grams

Dietary cholesterol

Eat less than 200 mg of cholesterol from food daily if you have high blood cholesterol levels, otherwise aim to keep your intake within 300 mg daily. Cholesterol is only found in animal foods, there is none in plant foods. The richest sources are egg yolks, organ meats (such as liver, kidney, and pate), and shellfish.

Exercise for your heart

Exercise confers many other significant benefits to the heart, including fighting the body's tendency to form tiny clots in the bloodstream— which can eventually coalesce into a larger clot that can cause a heart attack. Exercise also raises the good cholesterol fraction, the high-density lipoprotein (HDL) cholesterol, which protects the heart.

Boost your B vitamins

Eat plenty of folate, vitamin B_6 and vitamin B_{12} rich foods. These B vitamins seem to play a role in preventing artery-clogging heart disease. Researchers have discovered that people with high levels of a naturally occurring protein building block, homocysteine, are much more likely to develop atherosclerosis. While some homocysteine in the blood is normal, too much somehow encourages fatty deposits to form on arterial walls. Researchers have also discovered that people with higher levels of folate, vitamin B_6 and vitamin B_{12} tend to have lower levels of homocysteine in their blood. Thus, be sure to have a good intake of:

- Oranges and green leafy vegetables for folate
- Beans, meat, poultry, fish, bananas, and sunflower seeds for vitamin B_6
- Animal foods provide us with vitamin B_{12}. If you don't eat meat or dairy foods, you may need to take a supplement for this vitamin.
- Fortified breakfast cereals are often a good source of all these vitamins. Check the label to be sure.

I Spy: Finding the Trans Fats in Your Diet

Trans fats are often created when manufacturers make a liquid fat more solid, such as when they make a liquid vegetable oil into more solid margarine. Thus, many margarines contain this type of fat. Trans fats are also often used in processed foods such as donuts and cookies as they can have a longer shelf life. The process used to make the trans fats is called hydrogenation, thus you can watch out for these unhealthy fats by looking for the words "hydrogenated" or "partially-hydrogenated" on food ingredient lists. Some foods will also tell you they are "trans-fat free," or will list the amount of trans fats they contain on their nutrition information panel.

Boost vitamin C intake—but Naturally

This great antioxidant seems to play a role in reducing heart disease risk; this means it resists that harmful oxidation that can cause damage inside our body. In a study of 172 African-Americans, people with the highest blood levels of vitamin C had lower blood pressures (both systolic and diastolic) and also lower blood cholesterol. Remember those five servings of fruits and five servings of vegetables? If you harvest those for your eating plan, you'll be sure and get all the vitamin C you need.

Special Tips for High Blood Pressure

Here are a few nutrition tips especially for people with high blood pressure. We'll consider several minerals in our diet. Most people think first of sodium or salt but, as you'll see, it's only part of the story. Aim to eat a tower of minerals—at least these three important ones—to help keep blood pressure at healthy, lower readings:

- Calcium—Good sources include low-fat dairy foods and tinned sardines and salmon (of course, these fish are also rich in the precious omega-3 fats).
- Magnesium—Foods rich in magnesium include low-fat dairy products, meat, fish, poultry, legumes, and green vegetables.
- Potassium—Fruits, vegetables, and wholegrain foods are excellent sources of potassium.

Limit dietary sodium to no more than 2,400 milligrams daily. This is equivalent to about one teaspoon of salt. While it is easier to cut down on salt at home by not adding it during cooking or at the table, most of the salt in our diet comes from processed, canned, and convenience foods. Be sure to carefully check ingredient lists and nutrition panels to choose lower-sodium foods.

Special Tips for Type 2 Diabetes

If you have type 2 diabetes, eating a healthy diet, like the one at the beginning of the chapter, gives you your best chance to control your weight and your blood sugars. Remember that most people who develop this type of diabetes are overweight, and that losing excess weight goes a long way towards keeping blood sugar levels under control. Other important things include:

- Being sure to eat starchy foods such as bread, breakfast cereal, potatoes, rice or pasta at every meal. Choosing higher fiber or wholegrain types will help your blood sugar levels to be more even.
- Keep your sugar intake under control. While a small amount of sugar is acceptable in your diet, especially if your blood sugar levels are well controlled, it's important to avoid very sugary foods such as soda and Jello. Just choose the artificially-sweetened or "diet" versions instead. If you are having something sugary, the best time to have it is along with or just after a meal, so the small amount of sugar gets mixed with all the other food.

117

- Foods containing soluble fiber have a beneficial effect on blood sugar levels. Oat-based breakfast cereals, breads containing oat bran, and all types of legumes and pulses have this healthful effect.

Keep in mind that having type 2 diabetes increases your risk of developing heart disease, so also try to work some of the tips listed in that section into your daily life. Also, speak with your healthcare provider about guidelines for drinking alcohol.

Special Tips for Reducing Cancer Risk

Most tips for reducing cancer risk have been covered in the section on a healthy diet for everyone; as I said previously, that diet reduces our risk of a whole host of health problems. However, I think the information bears repeating:

- Control your weight—being overweight increases your risk of certain cancers.
- Don't eat too much fat, or too much meat or dairy food—a diet high in fat, especially animal fat is associated with some types of cancer.
- Choose plenty of fiber-rich grain foods, fruits and vegetables—as I mentioned earlier, there are substances called phytochemicals in fruits and vegetables, as well as certain vitamins, that seem to reduce our risk of developing certain cancers. In addition, a healthy fiber intake probably has a protective effect.
- Enjoy alcohol in moderation—excess alcohol intake has been linked with some cancers.

Putting it all Together

Many people with problems such as high cholesterol levels, diabetes, or high blood pressure will be on medication. Please don't rely on the medicine and forget a healthy lifestyle. Remember, even if your medical condition is controlled with medication, a healthy diet (including those essential omega-3 fats), exercise and keeping an eye on your waistline are all crucial to your wellbeing.

As you've seen throughout this book, omega-3 fats are an integral part of a healthy diet that combats a myriad of health problems, often helping to prevent them ever getting a hold on our bodies. I truly believe these miraculous fats have not only saved my life but help me to live my life to the fullest each and every day. Give your body the chance to experience this too. The next chapter is packed full of delicious recipes that are rich in omega-3 fats from both plant and fish sources. To help you put it all together, I've devised healthy, high-omega-3 eating plans for both fish- and non-fish-eaters. Flip to the next chapter and see just how delicious healthy food can be!

Chapter 8

Putting Omega-3s into Practice and onto Your Plate: Mealplans and Recipes

We've spent six chapters talking about how important it is to eat more omega-3s, where to find them, and even how to cook fish, use soy products, and soak dried beans. But if these items aren't usually a part of your diet, you may be wondering just how you're going to include them in your meals. I'm sure some of you can hear your children or partners now, saying that there's no way they're going to eat tofu, or that fish tastes boring. Well here's your chance to prove them wrong and do you all a health favor!

This chapter takes the nutritional priorities we've learned are so important and translates the scientific information into everyday meals and snacks. By looking at an overall healthy diet, you can also see that omega-3s are just one, albeit essential, component of a healthy diet. And this deliciously healthy diet is not just for fish eaters. Fully half of the mealplans are designed for those of you that don't, or can't, eat fish. Of course, those of you who do enjoy fish will benefit the most: you can indulge in all of the recipes and mealplans, whether they contain fish or not.

Using Our Mealplans and Recipes

Delving further into this chapter you'll discover four weeks of all-day mealplans for those of you who eat fish and those of you who would rather not. Of course there's no compulsion to follow the mealplans in the order they're given in the book; feel free to mix them up in any way you choose. There are also 35 delectable recipes, from salads to muffins to dinner-party-style salmon dishes, sprinkled throughout the mealplans. You'll know to look for these in the recipe section of this chapter because they're written in italics.

Obviously, because this book is all about promoting more omega-3s, our mealplans are quite high in this essential nutrient. You'll recall that the American Heart Association's recommendation for people without heart disease was two fish meals a week, with an emphasis on those high in omega-3s, and that people with heart disease would need to eat a meal containing oily fish most or every day of the week to get their recommended amount. Well the mealplans for those who enjoy fish include a high-omega-3 fish meal virtually every day, either for lunch or dinner, along with a good supply of the plant foods rich in omega-3s.

For everyone who doesn't eat fish, the suggested amounts of plant omega-3s for people without heart disease are 3 to 4 grams daily, and 10 to 15 grams for people who do have heart disease (though do remember that these are just estimates—no one is really sure exactly how much of the plant form is converted to the more valuable fish-type omega-3s). Our non-fish mealplans will satisfy your requirements whether or not you have heart disease; on average they contain a hefty 11 grams of plant-based omega-3s each day.

The wonderful thing about using mealplans is that they help you to form new habits, such as choosing lower fat foods, or using healthier cooking styles. However, of course, you won't want to stick with these mealplans forever. Just use them to establish the habit of high-omega-3 healthy eating, then follow your instincts and imagination! I'm sure that, even when you're not following the mealplans, you'll enjoy the recipes so much they'll become a regular on your dinner table, just as they are on mine. And to help you plan your diet, each recipe includes a nutrient breakdown, as does every day of the mealplans.

These recipes and mealplans differ quite a lot from the average American diet—they are much lower in total fat and saturated fat, and much higher in omega-3s. They are also a lot higher in fiber. If you usually eat the average American diet, and generally choose refined grain foods rather than wholegrain, you may find that your system isn't used to this amount of roughage. A good way to get your system accustomed to the greater fiber intake is to build up slowly, and one way is to gradually increase the amount of flaxseeds. These are one of the major contributors to the fiber in these mealplans, and there can be quite a few tablespoons recommended each day. I'd suggest starting with just one tablespoon and building up in half tablespoons from there. Along with a lot of fiber comes the requirement for plenty of fluid, which is essential to help the fiber to benefit your body. Aim for at least eight glasses of fluid each day, which can include any drinks that do not contain alcohol. Do try to make sure at least half these drinks also do not contain caffeine.

You've read all about the benefits of high-omega-3 eating, where this crucial nutrient is found, and how to cook the foods that contain it. Now, please move on to discovering the delicious side to omega-3s, and how enjoyable super-healthy nutrition can be.

Fish Menus

Day 1

Breakfast
Walnut Maple Hot Wheat Cereal with Flax
Juicy Apple

Lunch
Peanut Butter Banana Sandwich:
>   2 slices whole-wheat bread, spread with
>   1 tablespoon peanut butter, topped with
>   banana, in slices

8 ounces (1 cup) nonfat milk
Fresh orange

Snack
2 cups raw broccoli, with
2 tablespoons favorite salsa for dipping

Dinner
Garlic Roasted Salmon
Baked (small) sweet potato, topped
>   with 1 tsp. trans-fat free canola margarine, and
>   1 teaspoon brown sugar

1 cup green beans (fresh or frozen), steamed and spritzed with lemon juice

Snack
2 cups grapes

Calories 1626, Protein (g) 70, Carbohydrates (g) 245, Total fat (g) 53, Saturated fat (g) 7, Omega-3s (g) 9, Omega-6s (g) 13, Saturated Fat 7, Fiber (g) 48, Sodium (mg) 1115

Day 2

Breakfast
2 Banana Cranberry Muffins
8 ounces (1 cup) nonfat milk

Lunch
All Year Easy Tuna Pasta Salad, 1 serving
5 reduced fat baked whole-wheat crackers
Tall glass of ice water

Snack
Fresh pear

Dinner
3 ounces of grilled chicken breast
Baked medium sweet potato, with 2 teaspoons trans-fat free
margarine and 1 tablespoon chopped English walnuts
8 steamed asparagus spears

Snack
1 cup citrus sorbet, topped with 1 banana, sliced

Calories 1674, Protein (g) 83, Carbohydrates (g) 253, Total fat (g) 43, Saturated Fat (g) 6, Omega-3s (g) 6, Omega-6s (g) 9, Fiber (g) 28, Sodium (mg) 1297

Day 3

Breakfast
1 cup Egg Substitute, scrambled
1 slice whole-wheat bread, toasted
8 ounces (1 cup) nonfat milk

Lunch
Wrap:
    1 whole-wheat tortilla, ¼ cup black beans and
    ½ cup raw spinach, chopped, place bean and spinach
    mixture on tortilla and roll up
Fresh orange

Snack
1 tablespoon chopped English walnuts
2 tablespoons raisins

Dinner
Family Favorite Tuna Casserole
8 ounces (1 cup) nonfat milk

Snack
8 ounce nonfat vanilla yogurt, topped with 1 tablespoon almonds

*Calories 1606, Protein (g) 109, Carbohydrates (g) 216, Total fat (g) 40,
Saturated Fat (g) 7, Omega-3s (g) 2, Omega-6s (g) 9, Fiber (g) 23,
Sodium (mg) 2333*

Day 4

Breakfast

1 cup instant oatmeal, mixed with 2 tablespoons flaxseeds
8 ounces (1cup) nonfat milk

Lunch

1 cup mixed salad greens, topped with 2 tablespoons low-calorie Caesar dressing
1 cup red or green grapes

Snack

8 ounce nonfat vanilla yogurt, topped with ¼ cup frozen blueberries, thawed

Dinner

Ginger Seared Tuna, Garlic and Spinach
1 cup citrus fruit sorbet

Snack

1 apple, sliced, topped with 2 tablespoons chunky peanut butter

Calories 1466, Protein (g) 19, Carbohydrates (g) 204, Total fat (g) 43, Saturated Fat (g) 8, Omega-3s (g) 5, Omega-6s (g) 7, Fiber (g) 23, Sodium (mg) 1303

Day 5

Breakfast

Cinnamon Walnut Flax and Oat Bran Cereal

Lunch

Egg Salad

    3 chopped egg whites and 1 tablespoon light mayonnaise, with

    2 large romaine lettuce leaves

    2 slices whole-wheat bread, spread with egg salad mixture

Snack

8.25 ounce individual canned mixed lite fruit

5 100% stoned wheat crackers

Dinner

High Flavor Salmon Loaf

Snack

2 tablespoons dried cranberries

2 tablespoons raisins

2 tablespoons sliced almonds

Mix together 3 ingredients and serve

Calories 1734, Protein (g) 84, Carbohydrates (g) 224, Total fat (g) 64, Saturated Fat (g) 10, Omega-3s (g) 9, Omega-6s (g) 11, Saturated Fat 10, Fiber (g) 44, Sodium (mg) 2107

Day 6

Breakfast
1 Banana Cranberry Muffin
8 ounces (1 cup) nonfat milk

Lunch
2 slices whole-wheat bread, spread with 2 tablespoons
chunky peanut butter
8.25 ounce individual can lite peaches

Snack
5 baby carrots, with
¼ cup favorite salsa for dipping

Dinner
Roasted Tuna and Red Potatoes

Snack
8 ounce nonfat vanilla yogurt
4 pretzels rods

*Calories 1686, Protein (g) 86, Carbohydrates (g) 243, Total fat (g) 45,
Saturated Fat (g) 8, Omega-3s (g) 4, Omega-6s (g) 8, Fiber (g) 22,
Sodium (mg) 2526*

Day 7

Breakfast
Raspberry Orange Smoothie

Lunch
Wrap:

    1 whole-wheat tortilla, ¼ cup black beans and

    ½ cup raw spinach, chopped, place bean and spinach

    mixture on tortilla and roll up

Fresh pear

Snack
1 celery stalk, topped with 2 tablespoons roasted soy butter, sprinkled with 1 tablespoon dried cranberries

Dinner
Tofu and Broccoli Walnut Soy Sauce
Tall glass of ice water

Snack
4 graham-cracker squares, spread with 2 tablespoons roasted soy butter

Calories 1593, Protein (g) 55, Carbohydrates (g) 252, Total fat (g) 49, Saturated Fat (g) 7, Omega-3s (g) 5, Omega-6s (g) 8, Fiber (g) 40, Sodium (mg) 1306

Day 8

Breakfast
1 cup instant oatmeal, topped with 2 tablespoons raisins
8 ounces (1 cup) nonfat milk

Lunch
Tuna Pita Crunch

Snack
1 green bell pepper, cut into strips, topped with 2 tablespoons roasted soy butter

Dinner
3 ounces of grilled chicken breast, served on bed of cooked long-grain brown rice, mixed with steamed broccoli pieces, ¼ cup mandarin oranges
1 tablespoon sliced almonds, sprinkled on top of chicken breast

Snack
5 baby carrots
1 celery stalk
2 tablespoons reduced-fat sour cream for dipping

Calories 1511, Protein (g) 94, Carbohydrates (g) 189, Total fat (g) 46, Saturated Fat (g) 9, Omega-3s (g) 3, Omega-6s (g) 9, Fiber (g) 29, Sodium (mg) 1601

Day 9

Breakfast
1 cup egg substitute, scrambled
1 slice whole-wheat bread, toasted, with 2 tablespoons fruit spread
8 ounces (1 cup) nonfat chocolate milk

Lunch
1 cup mixed salad greens, mixed with 1 cup fresh strawberries, sliced
topped with 2 tablespoons low-calorie Caesar dressing

Snack
1 apple, sliced and quartered, topped with 1 ounce soy cheese

Dinner
Walnut Baked Halibut
8 ounces (1 cup) nonfat milk

Snack
1 cup red or green grapes, mixed with 2 tablespoons raisins

*Calories 1274, Protein (g) 87, Carbohydrates (g) 162, Total fat (g) 36,
Saturated Fat (g) 4, Omega-3s (g) 1, Omega-6s (g) 9, Fiber (g) 17,
Sodium (mg) 1154*

Day 10

Breakfast

2 *Banana Cranberry Muffins*

Lunch

1 medium baked potato, topped with 2 tablespoons roasted soy butter, steamed broccoli pieces sprinkled with 2 tablespoons soy cheese substitute topping

Snack

8.25 ounce individual canned lite peaches

Dinner

Hamburger:

    3 ounces extra lean ground beef, served on

      whole grain bun, with large tomato slice and romaine lettuce leaf

1 cup citrus fruit sorbet

Snack

5 baby carrots

Calories 1795, Protein (g) 75, Carbohydrates (g) 279, Total fat (g) 46, Saturated Fat (g) 9, Omega-3s (g) 5, Omega-6s (g) 6, Fiber (g) 27, Sodium (mg) 1710

Day 11

Breakfast
1 cup instant oatmeal, mixed with 2 tablespoons flaxseeds
8 ounces (1 cup) nonfat milk

Lunch
Egg Salad
    3 chopped egg whites and 1 tablespoon light mayonnaise, with
    2 large romaine lettuce leaves
    2 slices whole-wheat bread, spread with egg salad mixture

Snack
2 cups red or green grapes

Dinner
Lemon Sizzled Salmon Patties

Snack
8 ounce nonfat vanilla yogurt, topped with dried apricots

*Calories 1680, Protein (g) 83, Carbohydrates (g) 202, Total fat (g) 64,
Saturated Fat (g) 12, Omega-3s (g) 6, Omega-6s (g) 20, Fiber (g) 20,
Sodium (mg) 1946*

Day 12

Breakfast
Strawberry Banana Smoothie

Lunch
1 small whole-wheat bagel, cut in half, topped with 1 tablespoon chunky peanut butter

Snack
2 large stalks of celery with 2 tablespoons of salsa for dipping

Dinner
Main Dish Dinner Company Salad
8 ounces (1 cup) nonfat milk

Snack
4 ounce nonfat vanilla yogurt

Calories 2060, Protein (g) 150, Carbohydrates (g) 205, Total fat (g) 77, Saturated Fat (g) 13, Omega-3s (g) 15, Omega-6s (g) 15, Fiber (g) 32, Sodium (mg) 4653

Day 13

Breakfast
Walnut Maple Hot Wheat Cereal with Flax

Lunch
1 large whole-wheat bagel, cut in half, spread with 2 tablespoons and topped with 2 tablespoons raisins
8 ounces (1 cup) nonfat milk
Fresh orange

Snack
1 apple, sliced and quartered
1 ounce soy cheese for dipping

Dinner
Citrus Baked Halibut
served over a bed of cooked long-grain brown rice mixed with steamed broccoli

Snack
1 cup red or green grapes

Calories 1754, Protein (g) 89, Carbohydrates (g) 249, Total fat (g) 57, Saturated Fat (g) 7, Omega-3s (g) 8, Omega-6s (g) 17, Fiber (g) 44, Sodium (mg) 1024

Day 14

Breakfast
Power Peanut Butter Smoothie

Lunch
Whole-wheat bagel, spread with
    2 tablespoons roasted soybutter and
    2 tablespoons all-fruit spread
6 baby carrots

Snack
Pop-top (8.25-ounce) can of pears packed in juice

Dinner
Garlic Roasted Salmon
Baked potato, topped with chopped chives and freshly
ground black pepper
8-ounce (1 cup) glass of fortified low-fat soy milk

Snack
Banana, sliced and topped with 1 tablespoon chopped English walnuts

*Calories 1592, Protein (g) 65, Carbohydrates (g) 190, Total fat (g) 55,
Saturated Fat (g) 8.2, Omega-3s (g) 9.1, Omega-6s (g) 12.3, Fiber (g) 28,
Sodium (mg) 1024*

Day 15

Breakfast
2 Banana Cranberry Muffins

Lunch
Baked potato, split and topped with
    2 tablespoons soy butter, and
    1 cup steamed broccoli pieces (fresh or frozen), and sprinkled with
    2 teaspoons veggie soy cheese topping

Snack
Pop-top can (8.25 ounce) of peaches in lite syrup

Dinner
Hamburger:
    3 ounces extra lean ground beef, served on
    whole grain bun, with large tomato slice and romaine lettuce leaf
5 baby carrots with salsa for dipping

Snack
Sorbet Smoothie (1 cup low-fat, fortified soy milk blended with 1 cup fruit sorbet)

Calories 1795, Protein (g) 75, Carbohydrates (g) 278, Total fat (g) 46, Saturated Fat (g) 9, Omega-3s (g) 4.5, Omega-6s (g) 5.6, Fiber (g) 27, Sodium (mg) 1709

Day 16

Breakfast

One packet of instant oatmeal, mixed with

2 tablespoons flaxseeds, and

1 cup low-fat, fortified soymilk (all microwave until hot and smooth)

Coffee or green tea

Lunch

Egg salad sandwich, made with

2 slices whole-grain bread,

3 chopped egg whites and 1 tablespoon light mayonnaise, with

2 large romaine lettuce leaves

Tall glass ice water

Snack

2 cups red or green grapes

Dinner

Lemon Sizzled Salmon Patties

8-ounce container nonfat yogurt

Romaine salad, with 3 cups romaine lettuce, and 1 tomato, chopped, and drizzled with 2 tablespoons Balasmic vinegar and sprinkled with freshly ground black pepper

Snack

¼ cup dried apricot halves

Herbal green tea with lemon wedge

Calories 1679, Protein (g) 83, Carbohydrates (g) 202, Total fat (g) 64, Saturated Fat (g) 11.6, Omega-3s (g) 6.2, Omega-6s (g) 19.5, Fiber (g) 28, Sodium (mg) 1946

Day 17

Breakfast
Power Peanut Butter Smoothie

Lunch
Mushrooms and Artichokes with Edamame over Spaghetti

Snack
5 baby carrots with ¼ cup salsa for dipping

Dinner
Black Bean & Chicken Wrap, on a whole wheat tortilla with
  Grilled 3-ounce chicken breast in strips, topped with
  1 cup chopped baby spinach leaves
  1 ounce soy cheese
Kiwi, sliced and topped with citrus sorbet
Tall glass of iced seltzer

Snack
Pop-top can (8.25-ounce) of pears canned in juice

Calories 1590, Protein (g) 82, Carbohydrates (g) 187, Total fat (g) 48, Saturated Fat (g) 8, Omega-3s (g) 6, Omega-6s (g) 11, Fiber (g) 39, Sodium (mg) 1232

Day 18

Breakfast
Walnut Maple Hot Wheat Cereal with Flax

Lunch
6-ounces canned albacore tuna (canned in water), blended with
favorite mustard, and served with a whole-wheat bagel
Fresh apple

Snack
Fresh orange

Dinner
Lemon Garlic Greens and Tofu
Fresh kiwi

Snack
Hot fudge sundae, made with
    ¾ cup low-fat frozen yogurt, drizzled with
    2 tablespoons hot fudge chocolate topping, and sprinkled with
    2 tablespoons chopped English walnuts

*Calories 2150, Protein (g) 105, Carbohydrates (g) 328, Total fat (g) 57,
Saturated Fat (g) 10, Omega-3s (g) 10.5, Omega-6s (g) 18, Fiber (g) 48,
Sodium (mg) 1858*

Day 19

Breakfast
Whole-wheat English muffin, toasted and spread with
    2 tablespoons roasted soy butter
1 cup (8 ounces) Chocolate Soy Milk

Lunch
Basic #2: Take to Work Tuna Salad

Snack
Celery stalk, spread with
    2 tablespoons peanut butter, and dotted with
    1 tablespoon raisins

Dinner
Italian Roasted Salmon
1 cup cooked brown rice, sprinkled with freshly chopped parsley

Snack
½ cup fresh or frozen blueberries, topped with 8-ounce container of
vanilla nonfat yogurt

*Calories 1458, Protein (g) 80, Carbohydrates (g) 171, Total fat (g) 46,
Saturated Fat (g) 7, Omega-3s (g) 4, Omega-6s (g) 9, Fiber (g) 21,
Sodium (mg) 1827*

Day 20

Breakfast

Poached egg, served with one slice of whole-grain toast

1 cup (8 ounces) vanilla low-fat, fortified soy milk

Lunch

Easy Tuna Sandwich

8-ounce container of vanilla nonfat yogurt, topped with

    2 tablespoons chopped English walnuts, and

    2 tablespoons raisins

Snack

Herbal Green Tea Latte, made with hot green tea and ½ cup hot low-fat, fortified soy milk

Dinner

Grilled chicken breast

Apricot Rice Pilaf, made with

    ½ cup cooked brown rice

    ¼ cup dried apricot halves

6 steamed asparagus spears, spritzed with lemon juice

Snack

5 baby carrots with 2 tablespoons fat-free ranch dressing for dipping

Calories 1492, Protein (g) 62, Carbohydrates (g) 189, Total fat (g) 37, Saturated Fat (g) 8, Omega-3s (g) 3.4, Omega-6s (g) 10, Fiber (g) 24, Sodium (mg) 1806

Day 21

Breakfast

Packet of instant oatmeal, topped with

    2 tablespoons milled flaxseeds and

    1 cup nonfat milk (and heated until creamy hot)

Hot green tea

Lunch

Double Orange Albacore Lunch Salad

½ banana

Snack

½ banana spread with 1 tablespoon peanut butter

Dinner

Broiled pork chop

Baked sweet potato, topped with 1 tsp. canola margarine and

1 tsp. brown sugar

Spinach salad, made with 2 cups baby spinach leaves, and topped

with 2 tablespoons fat-free raspberry vinaigrette

Snack

Apricot-Almond Trail Mix: ½ cup dried apricot halves plus 1 table-

spoon sliced almonds

Calories 1798, Protein (g) 105, Carbohydrates (g) 222, Total fat (g) 57,
Saturated Fat (g) 11, Omega-3s (g) 6, Omega-6s (g) 10, Fiber (g) 30,
Sodium (mg) 1498

Day 22

Breakfast

Fruit Salad and Yogurt

    Fresh kiwi (sliced) and tossed with ½ cup grapes, and topped with
    8-ounce container nonfat vanilla yogurt, and sprinkled with
    1 tablespoon milled flaxseeds

Lunch

Balsamic Walnut Arugula Salad

1 cup (8 ounces) vanilla low-fat fortified soy milk

Fresh tangerine

Snack

Fresh apple

Dinner

Sweet Orange Garlic Salmon

2 cups steamed broccoli, sprinkled with minced red pepper and
spritzed with balsamic vinegear

Snack

½ cup sorbet, sprinkled with 2 tablespoons chopped English walnuts

*Calories 1734, Protein (g) 119, Carbohydrates (g) 189, Total fat (g) 67,
Saturated Fat (g) 12, Omega-3s (g) 10, Omega-6s (g) 15, Fiber (g) 28,
Sodium (mg) 1978*

Day 23

Breakfast
Cinnamon Walnut Flax and Oat Bran Cereal
Hot Green Tea

Lunch
Salmon Salad Sandwich
8-ounce container nonfat yogurt

Snack
4 thick pretzel rods
Tall glass seltzer

Dinner
Grilled 3-ounce chicken breast
Baked potato topped with 2 tablespoons nonfat sour cream
1 cup steamed green beans, spritzed with lemon juice

Snack
3 whole-wheat crackers spread with 1 tablespoon peanut butter

Calories 1776, Protein (g) 124, Carbohydrates (g) 190, Total fat (g) 60, Saturated Fat (g) 10, Omega-3s (g) 11, Omega-6s (g) 13, Fiber (g) 31, Sodium (mg) 2526

Day 24

Breakfast
Raspberry Orange Smoothie
Hot coffee or green tea

Lunch
Radicchio-Arugula Salad with Papaya Dressing
Iced seltzer water

Snack
Banana slices topped with 2 tablespoons sliced almonds

Dinner
Salmon Baked with Veggies
One cup brown rice, topped with minced cilantro

Snack
Petite trail mix:
    1 tablespoon peanuts with 2 tablespoons raisins
    8-ounce glass calcium fortified orange juice

Calories 1843, Protein (g) 79, Carbohydrates (g) 256, Total fat (g) 67, Saturated Fat (g) 8.7, Omega-3s (g) 10.5, Omega-6s (g) 23, Fiber (g) 45, Sodium (mg) 1102

Day 25

Breakfast
2 egg whites, scrambled in 1 teaspoon canola oil
1 slice whole-grain bread
Fresh orange

Lunch
Basic 2 Take to Work Tuna Salad
1 cup fresh grapes

Snack
2 tablespoons dried, sweetened cranberries

Dinner
Salmon with Tomatoes, Olives and Onions
1 cup (8 ounces) low-fat, fortified soy milk
Fresh apple

Snack
½ cup fat-free frozen yogurt topped with 2 tablespoons hot fudge
chocolate topping

*Calories 1611, Protein (g) 82, Carbohydrates (g) 198, Total fat (g) 48,
Saturated Fat (g) 10, Omega-3s (g) 4.3, Omega-6s (g) 7.6, Fiber (g) 23,
Sodium (mg) 1874*

Day 26

Breakfast
Walnut Maple Hot Wheat Cereal with Flax
Hot green tea

Lunch
Whole-wheat bagel, spread with 1 tablespoon peanut butter
1 cup strawberries, sliced

Snack
Banana

Dinner
Walnut Baked Halibut
6 steamed asparagus spears
Whole-wheat dinner roll, spread with 1 teaspoon canola margarine

Snack
One apple, sliced and spread with 1 tablespoon roasted soy butter

Calories 1598, Protein (g) 78, Carbohydrates (g) 203, Total fat (g) 60, Saturated Fat (g) 9, Omega-3s (g) 7.6, Omega-6s (g) 16, Fiber (g) 38, Sodium (mg) 1057

Day 27

Breakfast
2 Banana Cranberry Muffins
1 cup (8 ounces) low-fat, fortified soy milk

Lunch
Chicken wrap:
    Whole-wheat tortilla, topped with
    3 ounces chopped, cooked chicken
    ½ cup chopped spinach
    ½ tomato, chopped
3 tablespoons raisins
Iced seltzer water

Snack
1 cup grapes

Dinner
Crunchy Confetti Tuna Rice Casserole
1 cup steamed broccoli and cauliflower

Snack
Fresh pear, sliced, and topped with 2 tablespoons chopped English walnuts

Calories 1594, Protein (g) 84, Carbohydrates (g) 245, Total fat (g) 39, Saturated Fat (g) 6.5, Omega-3s (g) 6.4, Omega-6s (g) 14, Fiber (g) 29, Sodium (mg) 1757

Day 28

Breakfast

1 cup Fiber One cereal, topped with
    2 tablespoons chopped English walnuts, and splashed with
    1 cup low fat, fortified soy milk
Hot green tea or coffee

Lunch

Tuna Pita Crunch
8-ounce container nonfat yogurt

Snack

Cranberry Trail Mix:
    2 tablespoons dried sweetened cranberries, with
    2 tablespoons almonds
Iced seltzer water

Dinner

Salmon with Ginger, Spinach, and Carrots
Whole-grain bagel
Fresh kiwi

Snack

Veggie snack: 5 baby carrots and 2 stalks of celery

Calories 1550, Protein (g) 85, Carbohydrates (g) 205, Total fat (g) 40, Saturated Fat (g) 6, Omega-3s (g) 6, Omega-6s (g) 12, Fiber (g) 34, Sodium (mg) 1709

Non-Fish Menus

Day 1

Breakfast
Hot oat bran cereal:
> ½ cup dry oat bran plus 3 tablespoons milled flaxseeds, with enough water to cook

Lunch
Strawberry Banana Smoothie

Snack
1 small whole-wheat bagel, spread with 2 tablespoons creamy peanut butter

Dinner
Chicken Walnut Salad:
> 2 cups chopped spinach
> 3 ounces of grilled chicken breast
> 3 tablespoons chopped English walnuts
> 1 tablespoon olive oil

Snack
5 baby carrots, with 2 tablespoons low-fat ranch dressing for dipping

Calories 1789, Protein (g) 88, Carbohydrates (g) 205, Total fat (g) 77, Saturated fat (g) 11, Omega-3s (g) 11, Omega-6s (g) 18, Fiber (g) 50, Sodium (mg) 1385

Day 2

Breakfast
Cinnamon Walnut Flax and Oat Bran Cereal
Hot green tea

Lunch
Power Peanut Butter Smoothie
1 cup red or green grapes

Snack
2 tablespoons dried cranberries

Dinner
Mushrooms and Artichokes with Edamame over Spaghetti
Hot herbal tea

Snack
Banana, sliced and topped with
  1 tablespoon chopped English walnuts

Calories 1558, Protein (g) 68, Carbohydrates (g) 218, Total fat (g) 55, Saturated fat (g) 8, Omega-3s (g) 7, Omega-6s (g) 17, Fiber (g) 41, Sodium (mg) 984

Day 3

Breakfast
2 Banana Cranberry Muffins
8-ounces (1 cup) soymilk

Lunch
8-ounce (1 cup) low-fat lemon, coffee, or vanilla yogurt
¼ cup chopped dried English walnuts (stirred in)

Snack
1 small whole-wheat bagel, spread with 2 tablespoons creamy
peanut butter

Dinner
Chicken Walnut Salad:
   2 cups chopped spinach
   3 ounces of grilled chicken breast
   3 tablespoons chopped English walnuts
   1 tablespoon olive oil

Snack
5 baby carrots, with 2 tablespoons low-fat ranch dressing for dipping

*Calories 1695, Protein (g) 55, Carbohydrates (g) 243, Total fat (g) 66,
Saturated fat (g) 8, Omega-3s (g) 11, Omega-6s (g) 27, Fiber (g) 34,
Sodium (mg) 835*

Day 4

Breakfast
Cinnamon Walnut Flax and Oat Bran Cereal
Hot Green Tea

Lunch
Raspberry Orange Smoothie
4 whole-wheat crackers
1 cup red or green grapes

Snack
1 crème-filled chocolate sandwich cookie

Dinner
Lemon Garlic Greens and Tofu
Tall glass of iced seltzer

Snack
1 apple, sliced and quartered and topped with 2 tablespoons of dried
English walnuts

*Calories 1805, Protein (g) 63, Carbohydrates (g) 283, Total fat (g) 58,
Saturated fat (g) 7, Omega-3s (g) 12, Omega-6s (g) 19, Fiber (g) 58,
Sodium (mg) 684*

Day 5

Breakfast
Walnut Maple Hot Wheat Cereal with Flax

Lunch
Ham sandwich:
    2 slices of whole-wheat bread spread with 1-teaspoon dijon mustard,
    2 ounces of sliced extra-lean ham
1 apple, sliced and quartered

Snack
Fresh orange

Dinner
Balsamic Walnut Arugula Salad
Tall glass of iced seltzer

Snack
1-cup nonfat frozen vanilla yogurt, topped with 1 banana, sliced

Calories 1805, Protein (g) 63, Carbohydrates (g) 283, Total fat (g) 58, Saturated fat (g) 7, Omega-3s (g) 12, Omega-6s (g) 19, Fiber (g) 58, Sodium (mg) 684

Day 6

Breakfast
Power Peanut Butter Smoothie
Hot green tea

Lunch
1 small whole-wheat bagel, spread with 2 tablespoons roasted soy butter topped with 2 tablespoons raisins
Fresh orange

Snack
8-ounce (1 cup) low fat lemon, coffee or vanilla yogurt

Dinner
Tofu and Broccoli Walnut Soy Sauce

Snack
Fresh apple
3 milk chocolate candies

Calories 1703, Protein (g) 68, Carbohydrates (g) 234, Total fat (g) 64, Saturated fat (g) 13, Omega-3s (g) 7, Omega-6s (g) 13, Fiber (g) 40, Sodium (mg) 1586

Day 7

Breakfast
8-ounce (1 cup) low-fat lemon, coffee, or vanilla yogurt
¼ cup flaxseeds, stir into yogurt before serving

Lunch
2 slices whole-wheat bread, spread with 2 tablespoons chunky
peanut butter
8 ounces (1 cup) soy milk

Snack
3 tablespoons chopped dried English walnuts, mixed together with
2 tablespoons of dried cranberries

Dinner
Mushrooms and Artichokes with Edamame over Spaghetti

Snack
1-cup citrus fruit sorbet

*Calories 1712, Protein (g) 73, Carbohydrates (g) 228, Total fat (g) 64,
Saturated fat (g) 10, Omega-3s (g) 10, Omega-6s (g) 18, Fiber (g) 33,
Sodium (mg) 848*

Day 8

Breakfast
Walnut Maple Hot Wheat Cereal with Flax
Hot green tea

Lunch
Balsamic Walnut Arugula Salad
Tall glass of iced seltzer

Snack
Fresh pear

Dinner
3 ounces grilled beef tenderloin
1 medium sweet potato, peeled after baking, topped with
2 tablespoons dried English walnuts
2 cups chopped romaine, drizzled with balsamic vingear

Snack
2 cups red or green grapes

Calories 1624, Protein (g) 64, Carbohydrates (g) 201, Total fat (g) 72, Saturated fat (g) 11, Omega-3s (g) 12, Omega-6s (g) 26, Fiber (g) 26, Sodium (mg) 209

Day 9

Breakfast
Cinnamon Walnut Flax and Oat Bran Cereal
Hot green tea

Lunch
Radicchio Arugula Salad with Papaya Dressing
Fresh banana

Snack
Fresh apple

Dinner
3 ounces grilled pork chop, served on a bed of 1 cup cooked brown rice
2 broccoli spears, steamed
Fresh kiwi

Snack
1 *Banana Cranberry Muffin*
½ cup nonfat vanilla frozen yogurt

Calories 1846, Protein (g) 74, Carbohydrates (g) 256, Total fat (g) 69, Saturated fat (g) 9, Omega-3s (g) 13, Omega-6s (g) 24, Fiber (g) 48, Sodium (mg) 468

Day 10

Breakfast

1 packet of instant oatmeal, mixed with

    2 tablespoons flaxseeds, and

    1 cup low-fat, fortified soymilk (all microwaved until hot and smooth)

Lunch

Ham sandwich:

    2 slices of whole-wheat bread, spread with 1 teaspoon

    fat free mayonnaise,

    2 ounces of sliced extra lean ham, topped with 2 cups

    chopped raw spinach

    and 1 slice fresh tomato

12-ounces (1 ½ cups) calcium fortified orange juice

Snack

Fresh peach

Dinner

Hamburger with side serving of greens beans:

    3 ounces extra-lean ground beef, cooked

    1 whole-wheat hamburger bun, spread with 2 tablespoons ketchup

1 cup raw snap green beans, cooked, drizzled with 1 tablespoon

walnut oil, topped with 2 tablespoons chopped dried English walnuts

Snack

1 chocolate pudding snack cup, topped with 1 sliced banana and

2 tablespoons fat free whipped topping

Calories 1562, Protein (g) 68, Carbohydrates (g) 222, Total fat (g) 52, Saturated fat (g) 11, Omega-3s (g) 9, Omega-6s (g) 12, Fiber (g) 31, Sodium (mg) 2036

Day 11

Breakfast
½ cup Fiber One cereal, mixed with ¼ cup flaxseeds and 1 cup soy milk, topped with 1 cup sliced fresh strawberries

Lunch
Strawberry Banana Smoothie

Snack
1 cup red or green grapes

Dinner
Chicken Pepper Wrap:
    3 ounces grilled chicken breast
    1 red sweet bell pepper, sliced into strips and then cut in half
    1 whole-wheat tortilla
Place grilled chicken and red pepper onto middle of wrap and roll up to eat
Fresh orange

Snack
Power Peanut Butter Smoothie

Calories 1706, Protein (g) 92, Carbohydrates (g) 231, Total fat (g) 63, Saturated fat (g) 9, Omega-3s (g) 16, Omega-6s (g) 11, Fiber (g) 66, Sodium (mg) 851

Day 12

Breakfast
Multi-grain hot cereal:
Mix ½ cup dry oat bran, 2 tablespoons wheat germ, ¼ cup flaxseeds
And enough water to cook

Lunch
Bagel with fruit:
1 small whole-wheat bagel, spread with 2 ounces soy cheese
Fresh kiwi
2 medium stalks celery

Snack
1 Banana Cranberry Muffin

Dinner
Raspberry Orange Smoothie
Fresh apple

Snack
Caramel Sundae:
½ cup nonfat lemon, coffee or vanilla yogurt,
topped with 2 tablespoons dried English walnuts and
1 tablespoon hot caramel topping

*Calories 1809, Protein (g) 66, Carbohydrates (g) 322, Total fat (g) 49,
Saturated fat (g) 5, Omega-3s (g) 14, Omega-6s (g) 14, Fiber (g) 61,
Sodium (mg) 1144*

Day 13

Breakfast
½ cup multi grain cereal, mixed with ¼ cup flaxseeds and
6 ounces (¾ cup) soy milk
Fresh banana

Lunch
Chicken Breast Sandwich:
    2 ounces grilled chicken breast
    2 slices whole-wheat bread, spread with 2 teaspoons fat free mayonnaise
    1 cup chopped raw spinach

Snack
1 chocolate pudding snack

Dinner
Lemon Garlic Greens and Tofu
Fresh pear

Snack
1 cup chocolate sorbet, topped with 3 tablespoons dried English walnuts

*Calories 1701, Protein (g) 71, Carbohydrates (g) 266, Total fat (g) 50,
Saturated fat (g) 8, Omega-3s (g) 10, Omega-6s (g) 13, Fiber (g) 41,
Sodium (mg) 1170*

Day 14

Breakfast

8-ounces (1 cup) low-fat lemon, coffee, or vanilla yogurt
¼ cup flaxseeds, stir together with yogurt, topped with
1 tablespoon dried English walnuts

Lunch

Power Peanut Butter Smoothie
4 whole-wheat crackers

Snack

Fresh pear

Dinner

Beef Roast:
  2 ounces beef roast,
  1 baked medium potato topped with 1 teaspoon canola soft margarine
Salad:
  4 ounces raw arugula, topped with 2 thick fresh tomato slices
  and drizzled 1 tablespoon balsamic vinegar
1 cup chocolate sorbet

Snack

1 Banana Cranberry Muffin

Calories 1734, Protein (g) 74, Carbohydrates (g) 218, Total fat (g) 70, Saturated fat (g) 12, Omega-3s (g) 16, Omega-6s (g) 16, Fiber (g) 39, Sodium (mg) 809

Day 15

Breakfast
1 Banana Cranberry Muffin
8 ounces (1 cup) low-fat lemon, coffee or vanilla yogurt,
with 3 tablespoons of flaxseeds, stirred in

Lunch
Cheese Sandwich:
    2 slices whole-wheat bread, spread with 1 teaspoon dijon mustard
    2 fat-free cheese slices, 1 cup raw chopped spinach
2 cups red or green grapes
1 crème filled chocolate sandwich cookie

Snack
10 halves of dried English walnuts

Dinner
Beef Tenderloin Wrap:
    2 ounces beef tenderloin, broiled
    1 green sweet bell pepper, sliced into strips and then cut in half
    1 whole-wheat tortilla
Place beef and green pepper, onto middle of wrap and roll up to eat
1 cup cauliflower, cooked and drained, drizzled with canola oil

Snack
3 gingersnap cookies
8 ounces (1 cup) soy milk

*Calories 1719, Protein (g) 73, Carbohydrates (g) 236, Total fat (g) 64,
Saturated fat (g) 11, Omega-3s (g) 11, Omega-6s (g) 16, Fiber (g) 30,
Sodium (mg) 1668*

Day 16

Breakfast

Hot oat bran cereal:

½ cup dry oat bran plus 3 tablespoons milled flaxseeds, with enough water to cook

Lunch

Strawberry Banana Smoothie

Snack

Fresh apple

Dinner

Chicken Walnut Salad:

2 cups chopped spinach

3 ounces of grilled chicken breast

3 tablespoons chopped English walnuts

1 tablespoon olive oil

Snack

5 baby carrots, with 2 tablespoons low-fat ranch dressing for dipping

Calories 1390, Protein (g) 68, Carbohydrates (g) 158, Total fat (g) 60, Saturated fat (g) 7, Omega-3s (g) 11, Omega-6s (g) 13, Fiber (g) 41, Sodium (mg) 644

Day 17

Breakfast
½ cup Fiber One cereal, mixed with ¼ cup flaxseeds and 1 cup soy milk, topped with 1 cup sliced fresh strawberries

Lunch
Ham sandwich:
> 2 slices of whole-wheat bread spread with 1 teaspoon dijon mustard,
> 2 ounces of sliced extra lean ham

1 apple, sliced and quartered

Snack
1 crème filled chocolate sandwich cookie

Dinner
Mushrooms and Artichokes with Edamame over Spaghetti
Hot green tea

Snack
Fresh pear

Calories 1355, Protein (g) 65, Carbohydrates (g) 218, Total fat (g) 38, Saturated fat (g) 5, Omega-3s (g) 8, Omega-6s (g) 7, Fiber (g) 54, Sodium (mg) 1655

Day 18

Breakfast
Power Peanut Butter Smoothie

Lunch
1 small whole-wheat bagel, spread with 2 tablespoons roasted soy butter topped with 2 tablespoons raisins
Fresh orange
Tall glass of seltzer

Snack
8-ounce (1 cup) low-fat lemon, coffee, or vanilla yogurt

Dinner
Tofu and Broccoli Walnut Soy Sauce
Hot green tea

Snack
1 chocolate pudding snack cup, topped with 1 sliced banana and 2 tablespoons fat free whipped topping

Calories 1835, Protein (g) 71, Carbohydrates (g) 263, Total fat (g) 65, Saturated fat (g) 13, Omega-3s (g) 7, Omega-6s (g) 13, Fiber (g) 39, Sodium (mg) 1769

Day 19

Breakfast
One packet of instant oatmeal, mixed with
   2 tablespoons flaxseeds, and
   1 cup low-fat, fortified soymilk (all microwaved until hot and smooth)

Lunch
Raspberry Orange Smoothie

Snack
10 halves of dried English walnuts

Dinner
Chicken Fajitas:
   3 ounces grilled chicken breast
   1 green sweet bell pepper, sliced into strips and then cut in half
   1 cup broccoli pieces, steamed
   1 whole-wheat tortilla
Place chicken and vegetable mixture, onto middle of wrap and
roll up to eat
Tall glass of seltzer

Snack
1 cup of citrus fruit sorbet

Calories 1542, Protein (g) 74, Carbohydrates (g) 237, Total fat (g) 42, Saturated fat (g) 5, Omega-3s (g) 13, Omega-6s (g) 11, Fiber (g) 39, Sodium (mg) 705

Day 20

Breakfast
2 Banana Cranberry Muffins
Hot herbal tea

Lunch
2 slices whole-wheat bread, spread with 2 tablespoons chunky
peanut butter
Tall glass of seltzer

Snack
1 cup red or green grapes

Dinner
Balsamic Walnut Arugula Salad

Snack
Caramel Sundae:
 ½ cup nonfat lemon, coffee, or vanilla yogurt, topped with
 2 tablespoons dried English walnuts and
 1 tablespoon hot caramel topping

*Calories 1547, Protein (g) 49, Carbohydrates (g) 208, Total fat (g) 69,
Saturated fat (g) 9, Omega-3s (g) 9, Omega-6s (g) 26, Fiber (g) 29,
Sodium (mg) 1058*

Day 21

Breakfast
8-ounce (1 cup) low-fat lemon, coffee or vanilla yogurt
¼ cup flaxseeds, stir into yogurt before serving

Lunch
Bagel with fruit:
    1 small whole-wheat bagel, spread with 2 ounces of soy cheese
Fresh kiwi
2 medium stalks of celery

Snack
1 Banana Cranberry Muffin

Dinner
Beef over pasta:
    2 ounces beef tenderloin, broiled
    ¼ cup pasta, egg noodles, cooked without salt
    2 broccoli spears, steamed

Snack
Fresh pear

Calories 1289, Protein (g) 60, Carbohydrates (g) 200, Total fat (g) 35, Saturated fat (g) 7, Omega-3s (g) 9, Omega-6s (g) 5, Fiber (g) 36, Sodium (mg) 1107

Day 22

Breakfast
Strawberry Banana Smoothie

Lunch
Ham sandwich:
  2 slices of whole-wheat bread spread with 1 teaspoon dijon mustard,
  2 ounces of sliced extra lean ham
1 apple, sliced and quartered

Snack
1 cup red or green grapes

Dinner
Radicchio-Arugula Salad with Papaya Dressing

Snack
Banana, sliced and topped with 1 tablespoon chopped English walnuts

Calories 1445, Protein (g) 49, Carbohydrates (g) 240, Total fat (g) 44, Saturated fat (g) 6, Omega-3s (g) 9, Omega-6s (g) 16, Fiber (g) 41, Sodium (mg) 1344

Day 23

Breakfast
Cinnamon Walnut Flax and Oat Bran Cereal

Lunch
2 slices whole-wheat bread, spread with 2 tablespoons
creamy peanut butter
8 ounces (1 cup) soy milk

Snack
3 tablespoons chopped dried English walnuts, mixed together with
2 tablespoons of dried cranberries

Dinner
Beef Roast:
    2 ounces beef roast,
    1 baked medium potato topped with 1 teaspoon canola soft margarine
Salad:
    4 ounces raw arugula, topped with 2 thick fresh tomato slices and
    drizzled 1 tablespoon balsamic vinegar
1 cup chocolate sorbet

Snack
3 gingersnap cookies
8 ounces (1 cup) soy milk

*Calories 1815, Protein (g) 83, Carbohydrates (g) 214, Total fat (g) 77,
Saturated fat (g) 11, Omega-3s (g) 9, Omega-6s (g) 23, Fiber (g) 31,
Sodium (mg) 952*

Day 24

Breakfast
Multi-grain hot cereal:
  Mix ½ cup dry oat bran, 2 tablespoons wheat germ, ¼ cup flaxseeds
  And enough water to cook

Lunch
Power Peanut Butter Smoothie

Snack
5 baby carrots, with 2 tablespoons low-fat ranch dressing for dipping

Dinner
Lemon Garlic Greens and Tofu

Snack
1 cup chocolate sorbet, topped with 3 tablespoons dried English walnuts

Calories 1623, Protein (g) 67, Carbohydrates (g) 206, Total fat (g) 76, Saturated fat (g) 10, Omega-3s (g) 15, Omega-6s (g) 22, Fiber (g) 52, Sodium (mg) 896

Day 25

Breakfast
Raspberry Orange Smoothie

Lunch
Cheese Sandwich:
    2 slices whole-wheat bread, spread with 1 teaspoon dijon mustard
    2 fat free cheese slices, 1 cup raw chopped spinach
2 cups red or green grapes
1 crème filled chocolate sandwich cookie

Snack
Fresh pear

Dinner
Mushrooms and Artichokes with Edamame over Spaghetti

Snack
1 Banana Cranberry Muffin

Calories 1771, Protein (g) 64, Carbohydrates (g) 329, Total fat (g) 34, Saturated fat (g) 5, Omega-3s (g) 6, Omega-6s (g) 8, Fiber (g) 47, Sodium (mg) 1290

Day 26

Breakfast

½ cup multi-grain Cheerios, 2 tablespoons wheat germ,
¼ cup milled flaxseeds and 1 cup soy milk
Fresh banana

Lunch

Chicken Breast Sandwich:

    2 ounces grilled chicken breast

    2 slices whole-wheat bread,

    spread with 2 teaspoons fat free mayonnaise

    1 cup chopped raw spinach

Hot green tea

Snack

1 crème filled chocolate sandwich cookie

Dinner

3 ounces grilled beef tenderloin
1 medium sweet potato, peeled after baking, topped with
2 tablespoons dried English walnuts
2 cups chopped romaine, drizzled with balsamic vinegar

Snack

1 cup citrus fruit sorbet

*Calories 1200, Protein (g) 55, Carbohydrates (g) 159, Total fat (g) 43,
Saturated fat (g) 8, Omega-3s (g) 9, Omega-6s (g) 9, Fiber (g) 24
Sodium (mg) 370*

Day 27

Breakfast
2 Banana Cranberry Muffins

Lunch
Power Peanut Butter Smoothie

Snack
Fresh pear

Dinner
Balsamic Walnut Arugula Salad
Tall glass of seltzer

Snack
Fresh apple
3 milk chocolate candies

Calories 1530, Protein (g) 50, Carbohydrates (g) 188, Total fat (g) 74, Saturated fat (g) 11, Omega-3s (g) 13, Omega-6s (g) 23, Fiber (g) 42, Sodium (mg) 717

Day 28

Breakfast
Walnut Maple Hot Wheat Cereal with Flax

Lunch
Strawberry Banana Smoothie

Snack
1 chocolate pudding snack

Dinner
3 ounces grilled pork chop, served on a bed of 1 cup cooked brown rice
2 broccoli spears, steamed
Fresh kiwi

Snack
1-cup nonfat frozen vanilla yogurt, topped with 2 tablespoons chopped dried English walnuts

Calories 1802, Protein (g) 82, Carbohydrates (g) 253, Total fat (g) 60, Saturated fat (g) 10, Omega-3s (g) 12, Omega-6s (g) 17, Fiber (g) 37, Sodium (mg) 615

Recipes

The Breakfast and Snack Food

Banana Cranberry Muffins
Makes 24 muffins, which freeze well

1 cup applesauce
5 medium bananas, mashed
¾ cup packaged egg white
⅓ cup walnut oil
1 ½ cups brown sugar
½ cup plain nonfat yogurt
1 cup white flour
1 cup toasted wheat germ
1 ½ cups ground or milled flaxseed
2 teaspoons baking soda
2 teaspoons baking powder
½ teaspoon salt
1 cup dried, sweetened cranberries

Preheat oven to 350°F. Spray 24 muffin tins with vegetable oil spray.

Combine applesauce, bananas, egg whites, oil, sugar, and yogurt in mixing bowl; beat with electric beaters or by hand until smooth.

Blend, in a separate bowl, flour, wheat germ, flaxseed, soda, baking powder, and salt. Pour into liquid mixture and beat just until well blended.

Stir in cranberries.

Divide batter among 24 muffin cups.

Bake 20 to 25 minutes, or until knife inserted into the middle comes out clean.

Per serving: 212.4 calories, 34.5 grams carbohydrates, 5.1 grams protein, 7 grams total fat, 0.73 grams saturated fat, 2.12 grams omega-3, 211.3 mg sodium, 0.10 mg cholesterol, 4.4 grams fiber.

Cinnamon Walnut Flax and Oat Bran Cereal

Serves 1

1 cup original flavor, low-fat and fortified soy milk
3 tablespoons dry hot oat bran cereal
3 tablespoons ground or milled flaxseed
¼ teaspoon ground cinnamon (or to taste)
2 tablespoons chopped dried English walnuts
1 teaspoon brown sugar

Combine all ingredients (except walnuts and brown sugar) in a 6 to 8 cup microwave-safe bowl.

Cook at 70 % power for 7 minutes. Stir well.

Transfer to large cereal bowl and top with walnuts and brown sugar.

Per serving: 425.9 calories, 34.4 grams carbohydrates, 19.3 grams protein, 25.8 grams total fat, 2.4 grams saturated fat, 6.9 grams omega-3, 41.5 mg sodium, 0 mg cholesterol, 16.6 grams fiber.

Walnut Maple Hot Wheat Cereal with Flax

Serves 1

1 cup original flavor, low-fat and fortified soy milk
3 tablespoons quick cooking Cream of Wheat (or other hot wheat cereal)
3 tablespoons ground or milled flaxseed
2 tablespoons chopped dried English walnuts
1 tablespoon maple or maple-flavored syrup

Combine all ingredients (except walnuts and maple syrup) in a 6 to 8 cup microwave-safe bowl.

Cook at 70% power for 7 minutes. Stir well.

Transfer to large cereal bowl and top with walnuts and syrup.

Per serving: 455.8 calories, 46.7 grams carbohydrates, 17 grams protein,

24.7 grams total fat, 2.4 grams saturated fat, 6.9 grams omega-3, 44.7 mg sodium, 0 mg cholesterol, 13 grams fiber.

Power Peanut Butter Smoothie

Serves 1

1 cup original flavor, low-fat and fortified soy milk
2 tablespoons creamy peanut butter
3 tablespoons ground or milled flaxseed
1 teaspoon vanilla extract
½ to 1 cup ice cubes

Combine all ingredients in blender container; cover.

Blend on high speed until smooth. Serve at once.

Per serving: 426 calories, 21.1 grams carbohydrates, 20.5 grams protein, 30.9 grams total fat, 4.8 grams saturated fat, 5.5 grams omega-3, 189.1 mg sodium, 0 mg cholesterol, 13.2 grams fiber.

Raspberry Orange Smoothie

Serves 1

6 ounces firm, lite tofu (½ of a 12-ounce package)
2 tablespoons ground or milled flaxseed
1 cup frozen, unsweetened raspberries (or use fresh; if you use fresh, add ice cubes)
1 cup orange juice

Place all ingredients in food processor container; secure cover and process until smooth. Serve at once.

Per serving: 527.4 calories, 99.7 grams carbohydrates, 18 grams protein, 8.9 grams total fat, 0.92 grams saturated fat, 3.6 grams omega-3, 156.2 mg sodium, 0 mg cholesterol, 16.9 grams fiber.

Strawberry Banana Smoothie
Serves 1

6 ounces firm, lite tofu (½ of a 12-ounce package)
2 cups frozen, unsweetened strawberries (or use fresh, but add ice, too)
1 banana
½ cup orange juice
2 tablespoons ground or milled flaxseed

Place all ingredients in blender container; secure cover tightly. Blend on high until smooth. Serve at once.

Per serving: 426.9 calories, 76.3 grams carbohydrates, 17.9 grams protein, 9 grams total fat, 1.1 grams saturated fat, 3.6 grams omega-3, 159.6 mg sodium, 0 mg cholesterol, 14.7 grams fiber.

The Salads

Balsamic Walnut Arugula Salad
Serves 1, but can be multiplied as necessary

The Salad Ingredients
2 cups arugula, chopped
1 cup red tipped leaf lettuce
6 cherry tomatoes, quartered
1 carrot, shredded (or purchase carrot matchsticks in a bag and use about ½ cup)
½ cup edamame (green soy beans: purchase in the freezer section, and cook as directed, which is a matter of minutes)

The Dressing Ingredients
1 tablespoon walnut oil
2 tablespoons balsamic vinegar
2 teaspoons sugar
Dash cayenne
Freshly ground black pepper to taste
1 tablespoon ground/milled flaxseed

Arrange salad ingredients in individual salad bowl.

Whisk together the dressing ingredients in a small bowl; pour over salad and toss.

Per serving: 427.4 calories, 43 grams carbohydrates, 17.2 grams protein, 23.6 grams total fat, 2.3 grams saturated fat, 3.7 grams omega-3, 93.2 mg sodium, 0 mg cholesterol, 11.6 grams fiber.

Radicchio-Arugula Salad with Papaya Dressing
Serves 1, but can be multiplied as necessary

The Salad Ingredients
2 cups arugula leaves, chopped
2 cups radicchio, chopped
1 cup chopped broccoli
1 tomato, chopped

The Dressing
½ papaya, peeled and seeded
1 tablespoon walnut oil
1 tablespoon milled or ground flaxseed
2 teaspoons orange juice concentrate
Freshly ground black pepper to taste
2 tablespoons Italian parsley leaves

The Garnish
1 tablespoon chopped English walnuts
2 tablespoons golden raisins

Arrange salad ingredients in individual salad bowl.

Combine dressing ingredients in food processor bowl; attach top securely and process until smooth.

Pour dressing over salad and toss.

Sprinkle with walnuts and raisins.

Per serving: 452.2 calories, 58 grams carbohydrates, 11.3 grams protein, 23.6 grams total fat, 2.3 grams saturated fat, 4.1 grams omega-3, 75.4 mg sodium, 0 mg cholesterol, 12.2 grams fiber.

The Main Dishes

Lemon Garlic Greens and Tofu
Serves 4

1 tablespoon walnut oil
1 teaspoon vegetable bouillon paste
3 garlic gloves, crushed
2 cups diagonally sliced carrots
1 cup chopped yellow bell pepper
2 12-ounce packages lite tofu (1%) extra-firm, cut into 1-inch squares
4 cups arugula leaves, chopped
¼ cup lemon juice
2 tablespoons corn starch
2 teaspoons sugar
⅛ teaspoon freshly ground black pepper (or to taste)
4 cups cooked barley

Heat oil in large nonstick skillet with vegetable bouillon paste and garlic. Cook over low heat, stirring frequently, 5 minutes.

Add sliced carrots, yellow bell pepper, tofu, and black pepper. Cook, stirring occasionally, 3 minutes, until vegetables are crisp-tender.

Stir in arugula leaves; stir and cover for 2 to 3 minutes, just allowing arugula to wilt.

Blend cornstarch and sugar into lemon juice; pour over veggies and tofu mixture. Increase heat to high; stirring just until mixture thickens slightly.

Serve over cooked barley.

Per serving: 440.7 calories, 79.3 grams carbohydrates, 20.4 grams protein, 7.3 grams total fat, 1 gram saturated fat, 0.41 grams omega-3, 316.6 mg sodium, 0 mg cholesterol, 16.4 grams fiber.

Tofu and Broccoli Walnut Soy Sauce

Serves 4

1 tablespoon walnut oil
2 cloves garlic, minced
2 cups chopped raw broccoli
3 tablespoons reduced-sodium soy sauce
1 cup (about 1 whole pepper) diced sweet red bell pepper
1 cup chopped scallions (green portion only)
¼ teaspoon freshly ground black pepper
1 12-ounce package lite tofu (1% fat) extra-firm, cut into
1-inch squares
3 cups cooked brown rice, hot
4 tablespoons chopped dried English walnuts

Heat oil in large nonstick skillet or wok over heat; add garlic and sauté 3 to 4 minutes.

Add broccoli and soy sauce; increase heat to medium and stir-fry 2 to 3 minutes. Then add peppers and scallions, stir-fry 2 to 3 minutes more.

Stir in pepper and tofu; cover, and let tofu heat through (2 to 3 minutes).

Serve over brown rice, topped with chopped walnuts.

Per serving: 313.4 calories, 43.9 grams carbohydrates, 13.1 grams protein, 10.6 grams total fat, 1.2 grams saturated fat, 1.1 grams omega-3, 496.7 mg sodium, 0 mg cholesterol, 6.1 grams fiber.

Mushrooms and Artichokes with Edamame over Spaghetti
Serves 4

1 tablespoon dark sesame oil
1 12-inch peeled fresh ginger root, minced
4 garlic cloves, finely minced
½ cup minced onion
¾ lb (appx. 3 cups) sliced crimini mushrooms
¾ lb (appx. 3 cups) sliced shiitake mushrooms
¼ cup water
1 tablespoon reduced-sodium chicken bouillon granules
1 tablespoon fresh lemon juice (can use bottled)
½ teaspoon ground red pepper
2 cups artichoke hearts (canned, drained)
2 cups edamame (green soy beans: purchase in the freezer section, and cook as directed, which is a matter minutes)
2 tablespoons cornstarch, dissolved in ¼ cup water
4 cups cooked spaghetti
½ cup chopped scallions (green portion only)
½ cup shredded carrots

Heat oil in large nonstick skillet over low heat; add ginger and garlic. Cook, stirring frequently, 5 to 7 minutes.

Increase heat to medium; add onion. Sauté until browned; add crimini and shiitake mushrooms. Sauté 2 to 3 minutes.

Add water, the bouillon granules, juice, pepper, artichoke hearts and edamame. Reduce heat to low; simmer, stirring occasionally, 10 minutes.

Stir in dissolved cornstarch; increase heat to medium. Cook, stirring frequently, 2 to 3 minutes, or until thickened.

Combine spaghetti and mushrooms-tofu mixture in large serving bowl; toss to mix well.

Garnish with scallions and carrots.

Per serving: 478 calories, 76 grams carbohydrates, 26 grams protein,

10.5 grams total fat, 1.4 grams saturated fat, 0.4 grams omega-3, 107 mg sodium, 0 mg cholesterol, 13.5 grams fiber.

Main Dish Dinner Company Salad
Serves 1, but can be multiplied as necessary

The Salad Ingredients
2 cups baby spinach leaves
1 cup heart of romaine, chopped
6-ounce can pink salmon, with bone (drained)
½ cup marinated artichoke hearts, drained and chopped.
4 roasted red pepper strips (packed in brine, or freshly roasted at home)

The Dressing
1 tablespoon walnut oil
2 tablespoons dried and sweetened cranberries
2 tablespoons orange juice
freshly ground black pepper to taste
1 tablespoon chopped dried English walnuts
1 tablespoon ground or milled flaxseed
¼ teaspoon salt

The Garnish
¼ cup fat-free, flavored croutons

Arrange greens in bottom of individual serve salad bowl; add chunks of salmon.

Sprinkle artichoke hearts over salmon, and arrange red pepper strips on top.

Place all dressing ingredients in food processor bowl; place top on securely and process until smooth. Pour dressing over salad. Top with croutons.

Per serving: 1056.7 calories, 42 grams carbohydrates, 100.3 grams protein, 54.3 grams total fat, 9.3 grams saturated fat, 11.7 grams omega-3, 3858.8 mg sodium, 249.5 mg cholesterol, 10 grams fiber.

Double Orange Albacore Lunch Salad

Serves 1, but can be multiplied as necessary

The Salad Ingredients
2 cups baby spinach leaves
6-ounce can albacore tuna (canned in water)
1 cup mandarin oranges, drained well
¼ cup red bell pepper, chopped
¼ cup green bell pepper, chopped

The Dressing
1 tablespoon walnut oil
2 tablespoons orange juice
freshly ground black pepper to taste
2 to 3 tablespoons chopped cilantro
dash cayenne pepper

Per serving: 496.4 calories, 34.9 grams carbohydrates, 44.9 grams protein, 19.2 grams total fat, 2.7 grams saturated fat, 3.1 grams omega-3, 698.4 mg sodium, 72.2 mg cholesterol, 3.3 grams fiber.

The Sandwiches

Easy Tuna Sandwich

Serves 1

1 teaspoon walnut oil
1 teaspoon stone ground mustard (or other favorite mustard)
1 teaspoon fat-free Miracle Whip or mayonnaise
2 tablespoons chopped fresh cilantro
1 teaspoon sweet pickle relish
½ 6-ounce can albacore tuna, drained

2 slices 12 grain bread
1 cup baby spinach leaves

Blend oil, mustard, mayo (or Miracle Whip), pickle relish, and cilantro in small bowl.

Add tuna; stir well.

Build sandwich on bread, adding spinach leaves.

Per serving: 306.4 calories, 28.8 grams carbohydrates, 26.8 grams protein, 9.4 grams total fat, 1.6 grams saturated fat, 1.3 grams omega-3, 762.6 mg sodium, 36.7 mg cholesterol, 4.9 grams fiber.

Tuna Pita Crunch

Serves 1, but can be multiplied as necessary

1 carrot, grated
1 teaspoon low-fat mayo
1 teaspoon sweet pickle relish (optional)
freshly ground black pepper to taste
½ 6-ounce can albacore tuna, drained
2 tablespoons chopped dried English walnuts
1 whole-wheat pita, cut in half
2 large romaine lettuce leaves

Blend carrot, mayo, relish (if using), pepper, tuna, and walnuts in small bowl, using fork to break up tuna.

Stuff tuna mixture and romaine lettuce leaves into pita halves.

Per serving: 431.2 calories, 48.9 grams carbohydrates, 30.2 grams protein, 14.4 grams total fat, 1.9 grams saturated fat, 2.2 grams omega-3, 794.7 mg sodium, 36.1 mg cholesterol, 8.1 grams fiber.

Salmon Salad Sandwich

Serves 1, but can be multiplied as necessary

½ 6-ounce can pink salmon, with bone, drained
2 teaspoons light mayo or Miracle Whip
1 teaspoon stone ground mustard (or other favorite mustard)
2 to 3 teaspoons grated orange peel (fresh or bottled), optional
2 large romaine lettuce leaves
2 slices 12-grain bread

Blend salmon, mayo, mustard, and orange peel in small bowl, using a fork to break up salmon.

Build sandwich with bread and lettuce leaves.

Per serving: 494.1 calories, 27.6 grams carbohydrates, 50.8 grams protein, 19.1 grams total fat, 4.4 grams saturated fat, 3.9 grams omega-3, 1670.6 mg sodium, 128.2 mg cholesterol, 4.7 grams fiber.

The Main Course

Everyone's Favorite Tacos

Serves 4

1 tablespoon canola oil
2 teaspoons walnut oil
2 cloves garlic, peeled and chopped
½ cup chopped red onion
1 red bell pepper, minced
1 green bell pepper, minced
12-ounce package firm or extra firm lite tofu
½ teaspoon salt
1 teaspoon paprika
¼ teaspoon cayenne (or to taste)
1 teaspoon ground cumin
2 teaspoons sugar

4 flour tortillas
½ cup low-fat sour cream
½ cup chunky salsa
2 cups chopped red-tipped leaf lettuce

Heat oil in large nonstick skillet with garlic over low heat. Sauté an entire 5 minutes, releasing the flavor of the garlic into the oil.

Add chopped onion, peppers, tofu, salt, paprika, cayenne, cumin, and sugar. Increase heat to medium high.

Stir fry, adding a tablespoon or 2 of water as needed to create liquid as needed. Tofu will break up as it cooks, and spices will combine with oils and water to create the taco sauce.

Place ¼ of mixture on top of each tortilla; top with sour cream, salsa, and lettuce. Roll and eat.

Per serving: 310.9 calories, 42.8 grams carbohydrates, 13.7 grams protein, 10.1 grams total fat, 1 gram saturated fat, 0.63 grams omega-3, 804.6 mg sodium, 0 mg cholesterol, 3 grams fiber.

The Fish Main Course

Salmon with Ginger, Spinach, and Carrots (foil packet)
Serves 1, can be multiplied as necessary

4 ounces wild salmon (including skin)
1 teaspoon extra virgin olive oil
1 inch fresh ginger, peeled and minced
2 cups (⅛ pound) raw chopped spinach (bagged okay)
1 carrot, grated (or 1 cup carrot matchsticks purchased in a bag)
freshly ground black pepper to taste
2 teaspoons low sodium soy sauce

Place a large piece of foil on oven-safe baking dish with lip (to catch cooking liquids). Center salmon, skin side down.

Rub oil into salmon flesh; sprinkle with ginger.

Pile spinach and carrots on top; sprinkle with pepper and soy sauce.

Seal foil tightly; bake at 400°F for 20 minutes.

Per serving: 255.2 calories, 12 grams carbohydrates, 25 grams protein, 11.9 grams total fat, 1.8 grams saturated fat, 2 grams omega-3, 491.4 mg sodium, 60.4 mg cholesterol, 3.8 grams fiber.

Salmon with Tomatoes, Olives, and Onions (foil packet)
Serves 1

4 ounces wild salmon, including skin
1 teaspoon extra virgin olive oil
freshly ground black pepper to taste
1 Roma tomato, chopped
5 pitted black olives, sliced
2 green onions, sliced (top and bottom)

Place a large piece of foil on oven-safe baking dish with lip (to catch cooking liquids). Center salmon, skin side down.

Rub oil into salmon flesh; sprinkle with pepper.

Pile tomatoes, olives, and green onions on top.

Seal foil tightly; bake at 400°F for 20 minutes.

Per serving: 261 calories, 6.8 grams carbohydrates, 22.7 grams protein, 16 grams total fat, 1.8 grams saturated fat, 1.9 grams omega-3, 241.3 mg sodium, 60.4 mg cholesterol, 1.5 grams fiber.

Salmon Baked with Veggies (Foil Packet)
Serves 1

4 ounces wild salmon, including skin
½ cup mandarin oranges, drained

½ sweet green bell pepper, cut into strips
1 teaspoon dark sesame oil

Place a large piece of foil on oven-safe baking dish with lip (to catch cooking liquids). Center salmon, skin side down.

Pile mandarin oranges and pepper strips on top.

Sprinkle with sesame oil.

Seal foil tightly; bake at 400°F for 20 minutes.

Per serving: 296.9 calories, 24.3 grams carbohydrates, 22.4 grams protein, 11.7 grams total fat, 1.8 grams saturated fat, 1.9 grams omega-3, 59.3 mg sodium, 60.4 mg cholesterol, 1.5 grams fiber.

Sweet Orange Garlic Salmon (foil packet)
Serves 1

4 ounces wild salmon, including skin
1 teaspoon walnut oil
2 teaspoons brown sugar
1 teaspoon orange juice
freshly ground black pepper to taste
1 clove garlic, minced
1 cup frozen cauliflower
3 tablespoons orange zest

Place a large piece of foil on oven-safe baking dish with lip (to catch cooking liquids). Center salmon, skin side down.

Blend oil, brown sugar, orange juice, pepper, and garlic in small bowl; rub into salmon flesh.

Pile cauliflower on top; sprinkle with orange zest.

Seal foil tightly; bake at 400°F for 20 minutes.

Per serving: 285.3 calories, 21.1 grams carbohydrates, 24.8 grams protein, 11.9 grams total fat, 1.5 grams saturated fat, 2.5 grams omega-3, 84 mg sodium, 60.4 mg cholesterol, 5 grams fiber.

Garlic Roasted Salmon

Serves 1

4 ounces wild salmon, including skin
1 teaspoon extra virgin olive oil
3 cloves garlic, minced
⅛ teaspoon salt
freshly ground black pepper to taste
1 lemon, sliced thinly
1 tablespoon lemon zest

Spray baking dish with no-fat cooking spray.

Place salmon, skin side down, in baking dish.

Blend oil, garlic, salt, pepper, lemon zest, and lime zest; rub into salmon.

Bake at 400°F, uncovered, for 10 to 15 minutes, or until fish is cooked through.

Per serving: 228 calories, 8.9 grams carbohydrates, 22.3 grams protein, 11.6 grams total fat, 1.7 grams saturated fat, 1.9 grams omega-3, 345.2 mg sodium, 60.4 mg cholesterol, 1.8 grams fiber.

Southwest Tuna

Serves 1

1 teaspoon extra virgin olive oil
1 clove garlic, minced
1 tablespoon Balsamic vinegar
½ sweet red bell pepper, in strips
½ sweet yellow bell pepper, in strips

5-ounce bluefin tuna steak, including bones
¼ cup favorite salsa
1 cup snow peas, cleaned

Heat oil in medium nonstick skillet with garlic and vinegar over low heat, until garlic is wilted (but not browned).

Increase heat to high; add 2 tablespoons water, pepper strips and tuna. Brown each side of tuna—about 3 minutes per side.

Add salsa and snow peas; cover and steam until tuna is cooked through and peas are crisp tender.

Per serving: 377.4 calories, 28 grams carbohydrates, 39.2 grams protein, 12.7 grams total fat, 2.6 grams saturated fat, 1.8 grams omega-3, 349.4 mg sodium, 55.6 mg cholesterol, 6 grams fiber.

Roasted Tuna and Red Potatoes

Serves 1

5 ounces bluefin tuna, including bones
3 small red potatoes, skin on, sliced thinly
1 teaspoon extra virgin olive oil
freshly ground black pepper to taste
garlic powder to taste
1 small jar (7 ounces) roasted red pepper in brine, cut into strips
2 green onions, sliced (tops and bottoms)

Place a large sheet of aluminum foil in a baking dish; center tuna.

Arrange potato slices on top; sprinkle with oil, pepper, and garlic powder. Top with red pepper strips and green onions.

Seal foil tightly.

Bake at 400°F for 20 to 25 minutes, or until tuna is cooked through and potatoes are tender.

Per serving: 509.2 calories, 55.6 grams carbohydrates, 41 grams protein, 13.2 grams total fat, 2.8 grams saturated fat, 1.8 grams omega-3, 797.5 mg sodium, 55.6 mg cholesterol, 6.2 grams fiber.

Ginger Seared Tuna, Garlic, and Spinach
Serves 1

1 teaspoon dark sesame oil
1 inch ginger, peeled and minced
1 clove garlic, minced
2 teaspoons lemon juice
5 ounces bluefin tuna, including bones
¼ pound raw spinach (bagged spinach okay)

Heat oil in medium nonstick skillet with ginger and garlic, sautéing about 4 minutes to release flavors.

Add lemon juice and tuna; increase heat to medium high. Cook each side 3 to 4 minutes.

Reduce heat to medium low. Remove tuna to a plate; place spinach in bottom of pan and stir. Replace tuna on top of spinach. Cover and steam 5 minutes.

Per serving: 283.9 calories, 6.4 grams carbohydrates, 37.5 grams protein, 12.3 grams total fat, 2.6 grams saturated fat, 1.8 grams omega-3, 147.7 mg sodium, 55.6 mg cholesterol, 3.3 grams fiber.

Walnut Baked Halibut
Serves 1

5 ounces halibut, including bones (frozen okay)
¼ cup chopped red onion
1 teaspoon walnut oil
freshly ground black pepper to taste

Spray baking dish with no-stick cooking spray; center halibut in dish.

Place onions in small bowl; drizzle with oil and pepper. Sprinkle on top of halibut.

Cover with aluminum foil, leaving a vent.

Bake at 400°F for 15 to 20 minutes, or until fish is cooked through.

Per serving: 326 calories, 3 grams carbohydrates, 21 grams protein, 25 grams total fat, 4 grams saturated fat, 1.87 grams omega-3, 118 mg sodium, 67 mg cholesterol, 1 gram fiber.

Citrus Baked Halibut

Serves 1

5 ounces Alaskan halibut, including bones (frozen okay)
1 teaspoon lime zest
1 teaspoon lemon zest
4 thin lemon slices
4 thin lime slices
4 thin orange slices

Spray baking dish with no-stick cooking spray; center halibut in dish.

Mix lime and lemon zest; sprinkle on top of halibut.

Arrange lemon, lime, and orange slices, alternating by color and overlapping.

Cover with aluminum foil, leaving a vent.

Bake at 400°F for 15 to 20 minutes, or until fish is cooked through.

Remove rind from citrus slices, and serve fish with cooked citrus pieces.

Per serving: 299 calories, 8 grams carbohydrates, 21 grams protein, 20 grams total fat, 3.5 grams saturated fat, 1.4 grams omega-3, 118 mg sodium, 67 mg cholesterol, 2.2 grams fiber.

Italian Roasted Salmon

Serves 1

4 ounces wild salmon, including skin
freshly ground black pepper to taste
ground oregano to taste
ground basil to taste
⅛ teaspoon salt

Per serving: 156.8 calories, 0.45 grams carbohydrates, 21.7 grams
protein, 7 grams total fat, 1.1 grams saturated fat, 1.9 grams omega-3,
338.5 mg sodium, 60.4 mg cholesterol, 0.30 grams fiber.

Salmon Dip

Serves 6

14 ¾ ounce can pink salmon with bone, drained and skin removed
¼ cup reduced fat Miracle Whip
½ teaspoon ground dry mustard
¼ teaspoon cayenne
¼ teaspoon freshly ground black pepper
2 cloves garlic, chopped
4 green onions, sliced (tops and bottoms)
1 small jar (7.5 ounce) roasted red peppers, drained and chopped

Per serving: 149.3 calories, 5.8 grams carbohydrates, 14.9 grams
protein, 6.9 grams total fat, 1.4 grams saturated fat, 1.2 grams
omega-3, 615.4 mg sodium, 41.8 mg cholesterol, 1.7 grams fiber.

High Flavor Salmon Loaf

Serves 4

14 ¾ ounce can pink salmon with bones (skin removed and drained)
⅓ cup liquid egg white
3 tablespoons lemon juice

freshly ground black pepper to taste
4 slices 12 grain bread
4 green onions, sliced (tops and bottoms)
2 cloves garlic, minced
freshly ground black pepper to taste

Mix salmon, egg white, lemon juice, and black pepper with a fork, breaking up salmon.

Break up bread, add to salmon mixture with onions, garlic and pepper. Blend into salmon mixture with fork.

Spray a loaf pan with no-stick cooking spray; transfer salmon mixture into pan.

Bake at 350°F for 35 to 40 minutes, or until salmon loaf is set.

Per serving: 227.8 calories, 16.8 grams carbohydrates, 26.6 grams protein, 7.5 grams total fat, 1.6 grams saturated fat, 1.8 grams omega-3, 715 mg sodium, 58.5 mg cholesterol, 5.5 grams fiber.

Lemon Sizzled Salmon Patties

Serves 4

15-ounce can pink salmon with bones (skin removed and drained)
⅓ cup liquid egg white
¼ cup lemon juice
1 cup quick cooking (not instant) oats
freshly ground black pepper to taste
½ red onion, minced
1 green sweet bell pepper, minced
1 yellow sweet bell pepper, minced
1 tablespoon canola oil
2 tablespoons lemon juice

Mix salmon, egg white, lemon juice, oats, and black pepper with a fork, breaking up salmon.

Stir in onion and peppers.

Heat oil and lemon juice in large nonstick skillet or electric fry pan over medium high heat. Form salmon mixture into 8 patties; place in hot lemon oil.

Cook each side until browned, about 4 minutes.

Bake at 350°F for 35 to 40 minutes, or until salmon loaf is set.

Per serving: 300 calories, 22 grams carbohydrates, 27 grams protein, 11.5 grams total fat, 2 grams saturated fat, 2.2 grams omega-3, 623 mg sodium, 58 mg cholesterol, 3.4 grams fiber.

All Year Easy Tuna Pasta Salad
Serves 2

2 tablespoons fat-free Miracle Whip
1 teaspoon canola oil
1 clove garlic, minced
2 teaspoons lemon juice
freshly ground black pepper to taste
dash cayenne
dash dried oregano
1 cup cooked rotini pasta
2 cups chopped broccoli
1 carrot, grated
6-ounce can Albacore tuna, packed in water (drained)

Blend Miracle Whip, oil, garlic, lemon juice, pepper, and other spices in small bowl; pour over pasta and toss.

Stir broccoli, carrots and tuna; toss.

Per serving: 244.4 calories, 23.2 grams carbohydrates, 25.1 grams protein, 5.8 grams total fat, 1.1 grams saturated fat, 1.1 grams omega-3, 490 mg sodium, 37.1 mg cholesterol, 3.8 grams fiber.

Basic Take to Work Tuna Salad

Serves 1

2 cups spinach leaves (bagged okay)
1 3-ounce foil pouch Albacore tuna
8 cherry tomatoes
2 tablespoons favorite reduced fat dressing
¼ cup roasted soy nuts

Build your salad at home or at work—it couldn't be easier.

Per serving: 391.1 calories, 46.6 grams carbohydrates, 24.2 grams protein, 12.6 grams total fat, 1.6 grams saturated fat, 2.2 grams omega-3, 663.5 mg sodium, 35.7 mg cholesterol, 5.6 grams fiber.

Basic #2 Take to Work Tuna Salad

Serves 1

2 cups mixed salad greens (bagged okay)
1 pop top can favorite fruit (packed in juice), drained
3-ounce foil pouch Albacore tuna
2 tablespoons chopped walnuts

Build your salad at home or at work—it couldn't be easier. Wondering about the dressing? I've used fruit to wet your salad, and used the fat grams up in omega-3 rich walnuts.

Per serving: 345.2 calories, 35.3 grams carbohydrates, 24.1 grams protein, 12.6 grams total fat, 1.6 grams saturated fat, 2.2 grams omega-3, 368.9 mg sodium, 35.7 mg cholesterol, 5.4 grams fiber.

Crunchy Confetti Tuna Rice Casserole

Serves 4

4 cups cooked brown rice (instant okay)
1 can condensed cream of mushroom soup

2 tablespoons lemon juice

freshly ground black pepper to taste

2 cups frozen peas

2 6-ounce cans Albacore tuna, packed in water (not drained)

1 5-ounce can sliced water chestnuts, drained

1 red bell pepper, minced

Blend all ingredients, except red bell pepper, in large bowl. Toss gently.

Spray 3-quart casserole with no-stick cooking spray; transfer tuna mixture to dish.

Bake at 350°F for 45 minutes.

Garnish with minced red pepper before serving.

Per serving: 501.6 calories, 70.3 grams carbohydrates, 31.2 grams protein, 10.7 grams total fat, 2.7 grams saturated fat, 0.88 grams omega-3, 951.1 mg sodium, 36.9 mg cholesterol, 10.7 grams fiber.

Family Favorite Tuna Casserole:

Serves 4

4 cups egg noodles, cooked

¼ cup miracle whip light dressing

3 tbs. lemon juice

1 10¾ ounce can cream of celery soup condensed

3 cups peas and carrots frozen

2 6-ounce cans white tuna in water, drained

1 tsp canola oil

1 cup corn flakes

Cook noodles as directed on package.

Mix dressing, lemon juice, and cream of celery soup in medium bowl.

Stir in peas, carrots, and tuna; set aside.

Drain cooked noodles; place in bowl with veggies and tuna. Fold to mix. Place in oven-safe casserole dish sprayed with no-stick cooking spray.

Heat oil in medium non-stick pan; add corn flakes. Stir and cook for 2 minutes.

Place on top of casserole dish evenly.

Bake for 30 minutes.

Per Serving: 507.53 calories, 65.30 grams carbohydrates, 33.12 grams protein, 2.67 grams saturated fat, 1.04 grams omega-3, 2.63 grams omega-6, 1188.64 mg sodium, 101.48 mg cholesterol, 5.97 grams fiber

Index

Albacore, 79, 80
Alcohol, 112–113
Alpha-linolenic acid (ALA), 5, 7, 12, 90
Alzheimer's disease, 43–44
American Dietetic Association, xi
American Health Foundation, 44
American Heart Association, ix–x, xii, 9,
    12, 22, 25, 29, 30, 51–52, 79
Anchovies, 80
Arachidonic acid (AA), 7
Arrhythmia, 27
Artery-clogging process, 22–23, 26
Arugula, 94
Asthma, x, xiii, 36, 37
Atherosclerosis, 18, 23
Auto-immune diseases, 45–46

Babies, x, xi, 33–35, 40, 76–77
Baking fish, 85
Bass, 80
Beans, 97–99
Blindness, x, 49
Blood clots, x, 23, 24
Blood glucose, 25, 46, 117
Blood pressure, xiv, 15–16, 25, 27–28, 47,
    116–117
Blue fin tuna, 80
Body mass index (BMI), 106–108
Body weight, 106–108
Brain development, 8, 32, 33, 34, 40
Breast cancer, 44–45
Breast milk, 33, 34, 35, 76–77
British Medical Journal, 43
Broccoli, 96
Broiling fish, 88
Butter, 20
Butterfish, 80

Calcium, 117
Calories, 55
Cancer, x, 31, 40, 44–45, 90, 118
Canola oil, 21, 51, 93, 94
Cardiac arrest, 27
Centers for Disease Control and
    Prevention, 78
Children, xi, 42, 76–77. See also Babies
Chinook, 81
Cholesterol
    in blood, 17–21
        in diabetes, 47
        flaxseed lowering, 90
        genetic factors of, 22
        laboratory values for, 25
        omega-3s and, 26, 28
        types of, 18
    dietary, 17
        food charts of, 55
        reducing, 114–115
Chronic fatigue syndrome, 49
Clams, 82
Cold-water fish, 5
Colorectal cancer, 44–45
Coronary artery disease, 23
Crohn's disease, 31, 39
Cystic fibrosis, 37–38

Dementia, 43–44
Depression, x, 31, 41, 42–43
Diabetes, ix, x, xiv, 31, 46–47, 117–118
Docosahexaenoic acid (DHA), 5, 7, 12,
    33, 51, 53, 57

Edamame, 100
Eicosanoids, 8–11
    reducing blood pressure, 28
    reducing cancer risk, 45

reducing depression, 42
reducing inflammation, 26, 35, 36,
    37, 39
stopping blood clots, 24
Eicosapentaenoic acid (EPA), 5, 7, 12,
    51, 53
Elderly people, 43–44
Electrical system of heart, 26–27
Emphysema, 37
Environmental Protection Agency, 77
Eskimos, ix, 1–3, 25, 36, 38, 40
Essential fat, xi
Etretinate, 38
Exercise, 113, 115

Fasting blood glucose, 25
Fat intake, 108–109
Fetus, x, 8, 32–33, 76–77
Fiber, 56, 90, 112, 117, 118
Fish
    buying, 75, 81–82
    cooking, 75, 83–88
    food charts of, 58–61
    mercury in, 34–35, 76–79
    omega-3 fats in, ix, xii, 5, 58–61
    recommended intake of, 12, 29, 51
    selecting, 75–76, 80–81
    storing, 82–83
Fish liver oils, 52–53
Fish oils, 52–53
Flaxseed, 89–91
Flaxseed oil, 93
Folate, 56, 115
Food charts, 55–73
Fruits, 109–111

Grains, 71, 111
Grape leaves, 96
Green vegetable soybeans, 100
Grilling fish, 87–88

Halibut, 80
Headaches, x, xiv, 39

Healthy lifestyle, 105–119
Heartbeats, abnormal, 26–27
Heart disease
    artery-clogging in, 22–23, 26
    diet and, 16–23
    healthy lifestyle tips for, 113–116
    omega-3 fats reducing, ix, x, xiv,
        24–28
Hemoglobin A1C, 25
Herbs, 72
Herring, 80
High density lipoproteins (HDL), 18–21,
    25, 28, 47

Immune system, 45–46
Inflammation inside arteries, 26
Inflammatory bowel disease, 38, 46
Inflammatory disorders, 31, 35–40
Insulin, 46
Interleukin, 35, 36, 37, 45

Japanese villagers, 3, 9, 36

Kale, 95
Kidney failure, 47, 48–49
Kidney transplant, 48–49
King mackerel, 77

Land animal fat, 2
Leeks, 96–97
Legumes, 73, 97–99
Leukotrienes, 10, 36, 37, 39, 45
Lignans, 90
Linoleic acid (LA), 7, 14, 57
Low density lipoproteins (LDL), 18–21,
    22, 25, 28, 90
Low-fat diet, 108–109, 110
Lung disease, 37
Lupins, 97–98
Lyon Heart Study, 9

Mackerel, x, 80
Macular degeneration, x, 49

Magnesium, 117
Mahi-mahi, 78
Margarines, 93–94
Marine animal fat, 2
Meat alternatives, 100
Menstrual pain, 31, 39
Mental illness, x, 31, 40–44
Mercury, 34–35, 76–79
Migraine, x, xiv
Miso, 100
Monounsaturated fats, 4, 16, 17, 19, 20–21
Multiple sclerosis, 49
Mungo beans, 97
Mussels, 82

National Institutes of Health, 43–44
National Psoriasis Foundation, 38
Neurons, 41
Nuts, 62–64

Oils, 65–66, 93–94
Olive oil, 20, 21, 93
Omega-3 eggs, 34, 56–57, 89
Omega-3 fats
    alternative names for, 3
    definition of, 4–5
    in fish, ix, xii, 5, 58–61. See also Fish
    health benefits of, ix, x, xiii–xiv, 24–28, 31–50
    and omega-6 fats, 6–11, 12–13
    in plants. See Plant omega-3 fats
    recommended intake of, 12, 28–30, 51–52
Omega-6 fats, 6–11, 12–13, 21
Osteoporosis, 47–48
Oysters, 80

Pancreatic cancer, 40
Peanut oil, 93
Peas, 97
Phytochemicals, 110
Plant omega-3 fats, 5

vs. fish fats, 13–14, 34
    and heart's electrical system, 27
    recommended intake of, xii, 14, 29, 51
    sources of, 89–103
Plant omega-6 fats, 7, 13, 19
Plaque, 23, 26, 27
Platelets, 22, 24
Poaching fish, 85–86
Polyunsaturated fats, 4, 17, 19, 20–21.
    See also Omega-3 fats; Omega-6 fats
Postpartum depression, 43
Potassium, 56, 117
Premenstrual syndrome, 49
Produce, 67–68, 94–97, 109–111
Prostaglandins, 10, 33, 39, 45, 48
Prostate cancer, 45
Protein intake, 111–112
Psoriasis, x, xiii, 31, 36, 38, 46

Raynaud's disease, 49
Reddy, Bandaru S., 44, 45
Restenosis, 28
Rheumatoid arthritis, x, 31, 36–37, 46

Sablefish, 80
Salmon, x, 79, 80, 81
Sardines, 79, 80, 81
Saturated fats, 4, 16, 20, 55, 114
Sautéing fish, 87
Schizophrenia, 49
Shark, 77, 78
Sinks, Tom, 78, 79
Skin, 38
Smokers, 37
Sodium, 117
Soybean oil, 93
Soybeans, 101
Soy flour, 100–101
Soy foods, 69–70, 99–103
Soymilk, 102
Soynut butter, 102
Soynuts, 101
Soy yogurt, 101

Spices, 72
Spinach, 95
Steaming fish, 86
Stroke, x, 22–23, 24, 27
Sugar intake, 109, 117
Supplements, 52–53
    limited benefit for diabetes, 47
    limited benefit for psoriasis, 38
    need for, 26
    safety issues of, 25, 53–54
    taste of, 54
    types of, 52–53
Swordfish, 77, 78, 80
Systemic lupus erythematosus (SLE), x,
        xiii, 45–46

Tempeh, 102–103
Thromboxanes, 11, 24
Tilefish, 77
Tofu, 102
Trans fats, 20, 114, 116
Triglycerides
    and heart disease, 18, 21
    laboratory values of, 25
    omega-3s reducing, 26, 30, 47
    overeating and, 22
    supplements reducing, 52
Trout, 80
Tumor necrosis factor (TNF), 35, 36, 37
Tuna, x, 79, 80

Ulcerative colitis, x, 31, 39

Vegetables, 67–68, 94–97, 109–111
Very low density lipoproteins (VLDL),
        18, 26
Vitamin B$_6$, 115
Vitamin B$_{12}$, 115
Vitamin C, 56, 116
Vitamin E, 53, 56, 57

Walnut oil, 93, 94
Walnuts, 91–93

Whitefish, 80
Wholegrains, 111
Women, xi
    concerned about mercury, 76–77
    heart disease in, 15
    menstrual pain in, 31, 39
    osteoporosis in, 47–48
    postpartum depression in, 43
    pregnant, 8, 32–33
World Health Organisation, 35